# DRESSED FOR MINISTRY

*Izes Calheiros*

*To you*


*We all are in the School of Life,*
*learning submission to Christ.*
*As we learn it, He entrusts us with spiritual*
*authority and power to minister in His Church.*

*Learn the lesson as fast as you can—at any cost!*

*Izes Calheiros*

# DEDICATION

*To the innumerable women without ministry titles who are dedicated to the building up of the Body of Christ. To those men, with or without titles, who would like to fully understand God's purpose for those women. And to all members of the Body of Christ who desire to better comprehend the role of the church, as the Bride of Christ.*

# ACKNOWLEDGMENTS

I am very thankful to my dear professor of New Testament, Dr. Russell Shedd. After reading this manuscript he encouraged me to go on with the project by saying *"Sister, this may very well be what has always been in God's heart about women."* And then he proceeded to accept my invitation to write the preface to the original book written in Portuguese.

I am also thankful to Dr. Ralph Neighbour, who has been my mentor in the Cell Church vision, and with whom I had the privilege to work as part of the pastoral team of the Touch Family Church and the Touch Glocal Training Center in Houston, Texas. He read the English translation, and also encouraged me to publish it.

William Beckham is next on my thank-you list. He read it as if he were editing his own work. He made valuable contributions as well as asked many relevant questions that helped me to finalize it.

I could not forget the precious help of friends who voluntarily read and edited out of love and friendship: Mrs. Gail Curtis, from Abilene, Texas, and Caroline Hassel, from Houston, Texas.

# TABLE OF CONTENTS

# A WORD FROM THE AUTHOR

It was not in my plans at all to write a book about women in ministry. I was not even interested in books on the subject. I had consciously resisted engaging in the evangelical dialogue of the modern feminist movement. My sincere desire was just to please the Lord by fulfilling the pastoral and teaching ministry to which I have been called, without striving for recognition. I lived in that peaceful land until God started challenging me to speak on the subject in women's conferences and in evangelical newspaper interviews in my home country of Brazil. This book was born as a result of it.

I started by searching for biblical answers which could shed some new light on the ministry of women, hoping to contribute to the building up of the whole Church. As I got deeper into the research, the Holy Spirit led me to a broader understanding of the ministry of the Church as the Bride of Christ. The narrow initial purpose of learning about the ministry of women in the Church was transformed and expanded to reveal the woman as a figure of the Church of Jesus Christ. I had fresh insight on the understanding of the ministry of women, and men, in the Church since we are all members of the Body of Christ. That is what this book is about.

This book is not a feminist protest. It is an investigation of biblical texts on the roles of women and men, starting with Creation and advancing to the New Testament's teachings. I believe that going back to the beginning is the best way to move forward. So the biblical reflection proposed here returns to Creation to allow women and the Church to move on. This is a book for men and women. This is a book for the entire Church to learn how to please Jesus and how to grow in a relevant and powerful ministry to the world.

I urge you to ask the Holy Spirit to guide you through these pages, attentively examining God's Word with an open, free and inquisitive spirit. It is mandatory to take off any cultural, personal, familiar, social, historical and even theological preconceptions that may surround the topic of this book to be able to discern the pure biblical truth. The Bible teaches us that spiritual things are to be spiritually discerned (1 Cor. 2:14b; 1:17/18).

I ask God to fill all who read this book with a spiritual and profound understanding of what the Body of Christ is all about, that they may be able to understand the ministry of the Church and the ministry of women. I pray that many will be challenged to research this subject until the very core of the biblical truth is unveiled. Truth is the only worthy purpose of a serious and spiritual study of the Scriptures.

The time has come for the Church to know God's thoughts about the ministry of women, and to be able to advance in the establishment of His kingdom on this earth as one mature Body. May God be glorified in His Church by men and women alike!

*Izes Calheiros*

# PART ONE

# Part One

# The Foundation

Books, articles, conferences, and seminars have bombarded evangelical women in an effort to discover a position about their ministry that is biblical and acceptable to the Church. Tears, frustration, insecurity, bitterness, guilt, rebellion, control, rejection, and ministerial death have been associated with this slow and painful process. Miraculously, some women are actually able to fulfill their ministries with some recognition. But they are aware that they are not approved by all. Not having found the same favorable conditions, other women have been kept under the ministerial shadow of their husbands or leaders, trying to adjust to the adverse condition of ministry. This global scenario is in part because sectors of the Church do not entirely acknowledge the ministry of women. The concrete fact is that the Church has not yet reached a Scriptural consensus on this subject.

Reading, researching, reflecting and praying about it, I came to the conclusion that this occurs mainly because of misunderstandings of Paul's declarations on the subject and by a lack of discernment about what the Body of Christ is all about. Achieving an accurate and harmonious comprehension of these Scriptural concepts and verses will shed much light upon the issue. In the first section of this book we will lay four foundations to achieve such biblical harmony.

## Understanding the Order of Creation

It is necessary to understand the Pauline view on men and women to be able to comprehend what he means in each biblical passage. We must not conclude that Paul is a relativist or contradicts himself by giving different instructions to the Church according to their cultural backgrounds. We recognize the apostleship of Paul as legitimate, and the revelations he received as God's Word. And since the Word of God does not change, we can only believe that the apostle formulated his teaching from a consistent theological basis and then applied it within a cultural context.

Searching the Scriptures, I came to understand that this theological basis is called "the order of creation." This order of creation taken together with Paul's teaching on the Body of Christ will clarify the role of women in the family, in Church and in society. We will begin with this foundation and build on it step by step with the apostle's teachings, until we reach a sound and biblical conclusion. This will hopefully lead the Church to take a definitive and indisputable position about this issue. We will also examine the woman as a figure of the Church and draw some important conclusions for the ministry of women, men, and of the Church.

I pray that this book will be powerful in breaking down the chains that are imprisoning a large number of women across the world and keeping them from fulfilling their God-appointed ministries. I also hope that the men who read this book will gain a greater understanding of the ministry of their sisters in Christ; and, as a result, they will become instruments of God to unchain the women in the Body of Christ, "until we all reach unity in the faith and in the knowledge of the Son of God and become mature, attaining to the whole measure of the fullness of Christ" (Eph. 4:13).

## Understanding the Body of Christ

*Then we will no longer be infants, tossed back and forth by the waves, and blown here and there by every wind of teaching and by the cunning and craftiness of men in their deceitful scheming. Instead, speaking the truth in love, we will in all things grow up into Him who is the Head, that is, Christ. From him the whole body, joined and held together by every supporting ligament, grows and builds itself up in love, as each part does its work* (Eph. 4: 14-16).

Doesn't this text sound like a dream? Paul is talking about the mature and grown up Church. The mature man in this text is one formed by the union of the Risen Christ, who is seated at the right hand of God as the Head of the Church, and His Body, the Church, also seated with Him. Christ who is seated in the heavenly places today has the Church with Him. He is not alone anymore. The Church was baptized into His death, and raised with Him in His resurrection. Christ is the HEAD united to His BODY. Paul explained it this way to the Church at Ephesus:

*But because of His great love for us, God, who is rich in mercy, made us alive with Christ even when we were dead in transgressions—it is by grace you have been saved. And God raised us up with Christ and seated us with him in the heavenly realms in Christ Jesus, in order that in the coming ages he might show the incomparable riches of his grace, expressed in his kindness to us in Christ Jesus* (Eph. 2:4-7).

The revelation that Paul has about the Church as the complementary Body of Christ is not just for heaven. It is also for the here and now. When the whole Church grows in this understanding and practice of the unity of this Body with Him, it will be a mature Church. The Church is not divided into many parts. It is a whole and complete unit, made up of many parts. Since the Holy Spirit has baptized us into one Body, it does not matter any more if we are Jews or Greeks, slave or free, male or female, because now we are all one in Christ. This is a revelation to be spiritually discerned, and the following passages help us do that.

> *The body is a unit, though it is made up of many parts; and though all its parts are many, they form one body. So it is with Christ. For we were all baptized by one Spirit into one body—whether Jews or Greeks, slave or free—and we were all given the one Spirit to drink (1 Cor. 12:12, 13).*

> *You are all sons of God through faith in Christ Jesus, for all of you who were baptized into Christ have clothed yourselves with Christ. There is neither Jew nor Greek, slave nor free, male nor female, for you are all one in Christ Jesus (Gal. 3:26-28).*

> *I pray also that the eyes of your heart may be enlightened in order that you may know the hope to which he has called you, the riches of his glorious inheritance in the saints, and his incomparably great power for us who believe. That power is like the working of his mighty strength, which he exerted in Christ when he raised him from the dead and seated him at his right hand in the heavenly realms, far above all rule and authority, power and dominion, and every title that can be given, not only in the present age but also in*

*the one to come. And God placed all things under his feet and appointed him to be head over everything for the Church, which is his body, the fullness of him who fills everything in every way* (Eph. 1:18-23).

*Now you are the body of Christ, and each one of you is a part of it* (1 Cor. 12:27).

*Here there is no Greek or Jew, circumcised or uncircumcised, barbarian, Scythian, slave or free, but Christ is all, and is in all.* (Col. 3:11).

After centuries fighting against social and cultural boundaries, the Church has put down the wall of separation between Jews and Gentiles, has put away ritualistic circumcision, has freed the slaves and has forgiven the barbarians. Sadly, it has not yet set women free from bondage in Church ministry. The truth is that by the third millennium the female part of the Body of Christ is still in slavery, and that, in a way, keeps Christ in bondage. The Church cannot afford to move on with only one half of the Body of Christ because the other half is in chains. It is time to change history and set the Church free.

Does Jesus need to do additional redemptive work for that to happen? Aren't His last words *it is finished* and the power of His resurrected life sufficient? Has He forgotten any part of His duties and tasks commanded by the Father? Would He need to return to earth and die again just to please some that have hardened their hearts and want to promote division instead of unity in the Body of Christ? That seems to be the case for those who lack spiritual discernment about the Body of Christ; those who keep in slavery the part of Christ's Body made up of women. As they do so, they put Christ in bondage and make Him, the Head of His Church, to be subjected to men.

*These are the men who divide you, who follow mere natural instincts and do not have the Spirit* (Jude 1:19).

## Understanding the Biblical Meaning of Submission

Submission has been the subject of many questions and discussions for centuries. I guarantee it is not a favorite word for women. Innumerable women have been hurt for too long by the way this word has been interpreted and applied in real life. Throughout history, many have misunderstood submission, men as well as women. It has been misused and misinterpreted through the centuries in a way that has favored and enhanced male abuse and dominance. Nothing could be further from God's heart than that kind of interpretation.

Maybe we should come up with a different word. But, isn't it "submission" the word God chose? Men have reinterpreted it. Some of them did it thinking they were pleasing God. The question is how do we restore the beautiful biblical meaning of this word? Is it possible to restore it? This is one of the purposes of this book.

The biblical meaning of the word is quite different from its general use. We will have to approach this word as if we were learning a new language. Let's do so.

Submission must be understood exactly as the text reads. Paul used a Greek word taken from architectural vocabulary. The word is *hypotasimos*, and it represents a paradigm in a house where everyone is a servant (*doulos*) to one other (Eph. 5:21). *Hypotasimos* used in the above passage could refer to a support used for the building of a bridge. It should be translated as "to live in mutual support," serving one another. The amplified meaning is: everything done in the home should support the edification, harmony, and unity of the couples' mission and purpose in life. It means that everyone should fit into the function and position to which they are called.

Submission should never be understood as a way to oppress, to control or to despise women and their contribution to family, Church, society and life in general. This wrong conception of submission originates in the arrogance and pride of the human spirit.

Submission in the Kingdom of God is different from the way the world understands and applies it. Was Jesus submissive to the Father? Did the Father impose His Will on Jesus? Was Jesus offended by the Father staying in heaven in a position of authority while He came to suffer in the world? Was Jesus inferior to the Father because He was the one who had to come to the world and had to obey the Father? Wasn't that the agreement made before the world was made that they would work together to accomplish such mission? Wasn't it just a matter of the "order of things"?

The apostle Paul states very clearly that in the Church we should submit to one another. That is the way things are in the kingdom. How do we submit to one another in the Church? That is a very important question, which is fully answered in another chapter in this book. But, as a preview to that chapter, it is necessary to understand at this point that submission in the Church is related to the order of things established by Jesus as the Head of the Church and by the Holy Spirit who is with the Church to guide her into all truth. There is an order at work in the Church and that is the order of the Holy Spirit. It is not an order established by men or women, or pastors, or teachers, or apostles, even if they hold an important title in the Church. Ultimately, submission is due to God.

I like the explanation offered by Lynette Hoy, in the article *Should Wives Really Submit?*

*Submission is a word which can be described as "willing conciliation." That means that the wife should be "willing," not coerced. Wives are to*

*respect their husbands. Husbands are to be consider-*
*ate of their wives. Both partners should be willing*
*to "put the other's interests above his/her own"*
*as Philippians 2 describes. The woman should be*
*willing to submit to her husband not be unwilling or*
*forced. The man should be a loving, servant leader*
*– accountable and responsible to God and his family.*
*A loving leader leads –doesn't manipulate or pres-*
*sure. A submitter doesn't "take over."*

## Understanding the Meaning of Spiritual Leadership

It is very important to clarify what spiritual leadership means. Jesus was the first to talk about it in the New
Testament. According to His teaching, leadership in the
Kingdom of God contrasts with the concept of leadership in
the world and in the kingdom of men.

*Jesus called them together and said, "You know that*
*the rulers of the Gentiles lord it over them, and their*
*high officials exercise authority over them. Not so*
*with you. Instead, whoever wants to become great*
*among you must be your servant, and whoever wants*
*to be first must be your slave— just as the Son of Man*
*did not come to be served, but to serve, and to give*
*his life as a ransom for many* (Mat. 20: 25-28).

Kingdom leadership is different. I am so glad that our
Lord Jesus Christ clarified it for us and set the example
for us to follow. This model works well for everything in
His kingdom, including the Church, the family, Mission
Agencies, Christian Schools, Seminaries, businesses, etc.
That is the model Jesus Christ set up for Himself in order to
be the Head of the Church, that is, His Bride. Every man is
supposed to follow Christ's example in leading his family.

He is not to "lord it over his wife," but to "serve her." What a spectacular concept of leadership and government.

In a practical way, a husband's leadership task could be described as a facilitator of the couple's mission in order to understand Christ's mind for the family. As such, he leads the family with the spiritual authority that comes directly from Jesus, as he follows His commandments and directions in his personal life. It is from Jesus Christ that his leadership comes. It is not from himself per se. He is given by God a natural gift of government and the spiritual authority from Christ to lead the family.

## Chapter One

# The Perfect Ecology of Eden

To understand the ministry of women for today's church, it is necessary to travel back to the origin of all things and take a close look at some special conditions in place during the creation of man and woman. Herein lies the foundation of this biblical construction — the order of creation.

### Creation as the Starting Point

It is fundamental, as well as urgent, to take Creation as the starting point in order to bring healing to the church and restoration of the ministry of millions of women who are members of the Body of Christ. This will also release men from the bondage of control and oppression. From this perspective, we should know Adam and Eve better, by taking a view of the environment where they were created and lived. There is no better description of the ecological paradise that was their home than the biblical account:

*This is the account of the heavens and the earth when they were created. When the LORD God made the earth and the heavens— and no shrub of the field had yet appeared on the earth and no plant of the field had yet sprung up, for the LORD God had not sent rain on the earth and there was no man to work the ground, but streams came up from the earth and watered the whole surface of the ground— the LORD God formed the man from the dust of the ground and breathed into his nostrils the breath of life, and the man became a living being. Now the LORD God had planted a garden in the east, in Eden; and there he put the man he had formed. And the LORD God made all kinds of trees grow out of the ground—trees that were pleasing to the eye and good for food. In the middle of the garden were the tree of life and the tree of the knowledge of good and evil The LORD God took the man and put him in the Garden of Eden to work it and take care of it* (Gen. 2:4-9, 15).

The passage describes with rare beauty the origin of everything that was created, showing the position and the responsibility given to man over all the creation of God. At that point the woman was still to be created. Since the beginning, the relationship between God and man has been primarily of a spiritual order, and secondarily of an earthly order (Gen. 1:26-28).

From the Lord, who gave man physical and spiritual life, Adam received a commandment to administer the garden and to develop the land. Adam started well in his relationship with his Lord, learning how to live in obedience to Him. He also had a good start with the animals, to which he gave appropriate names, demonstrating that he was given a position of peaceful ruling over them. His relationship to the soil could not be better. The earth gave him all the fruits he needed for food easily and in abundance (Gen. 1:28-30).

Besides that, Adam was established as the guardian of the Garden of Eden (Gen.2:15). He spoke daily with God,

listened to His voice, and enjoyed His presence and fellowship (Gen. 3:8). He was loved by God and crowned with
glory and honor, as the psalmist declares:

> *You made him a little lower than the heavenly beings*
> *and crowned him with glory and honor. You made*
> *him ruler over the works of your hands; you put*
> *everything under his feet: all flocks and herds, and*
> *the beasts of the field, the birds of the air, and the fish*
> *of the sea, and all that swim the paths of the seas* (Ps.
> 8: 5-8).

## Something is missing in the Paradise of Eden

In this relational ecology, everything was working out
well with the soil, with the animals, and with God. Adam
received a very precise commandment which had the
purpose of preserving the ecological equilibrium that would
guarantee the progress of life on earth:

> *And the LORD God commanded the man, "You are*
> *free to eat from any tree in the garden; but you must*
> *not eat from the tree of the knowledge of good and*
> *evil, for when you eat of it you will surely die* (Gen.
> 2:16-17).

God was making an alliance with Adam— the Edenic
covenant. In words, the Creator was giving him a direct
order: "choose life instead of death". Adam was expected to
make a spiritual decision that was not related to the physical
need for food. In the garden, the first man had everything he
needed to be well fed. He was supposed to make a unique
decision which would have spiritual and eternal consequences: to eat from the tree of life, freely accessible to him,

and choose life; or to eat from the tree of the knowledge of good and evil, prohibited to him, and choose death.

Adam did not know yet, but he was learning how to walk in submission to God in the Garden of Eden School. This apprenticeship would prepare him to exercise spiritual authority in the family God was about to form. Up to that point, there are no indications that Adam had already eaten from the tree of life. If he had done so, he would have been judged to live forever far from God, after the sin he was about to commit. If that had been the case, the disaster to all humanity would have been eternally fatal.

God brought the animals He had created for Adam to name them:

*So the man gave names to all the livestock, the birds of the air and all the beasts of the field. But for Adam no suitable helper was found* (Gen. 2:20).

Almost everything was satisfactory in that earthly paradise. But Adam was missing something. He felt the need to have someone like him who would relate to him in a personal and intimate way. Adam needed someone who would fulfill him and who would be suitable to help him accomplish the phenomenal God-given mission and responsibility.

### The Perfect Ecology of Eden

God was sensitive and attentive to that important man's need, and in the sixth day of creation, as He concluded His majestic work, He made this remarkable declaration:

*It is not good for the man to be alone. I will make a helper suitable for him* (Gen. 2.18).

By God's decision, and for the joy of the man, the first woman is brought into existence. The woman was the missing element in the garden and in Adam's life. The nature of God's declaration about the woman is very profound and reveals how much Adam was in *need* of her (it is not good for the man to be alone); the *importance* of the role she would have in his life (I will make him a helper); and the level of her *competence* (suitable for him). It is notable that God considers the woman necessary, important, and appropriate for the man as well as for the accomplishment of His purpose on earth. It is lamentable that not everyone has yet achieved this understanding based on the creation account alone.

The order of creation described in Genesis 2 is clear: God created Adam first, and then He created Eve. The Lord brought her into existence because of him, to play an important role in his life and for them to accomplish together God's purpose for life on earth. Her creation made perfect the ecological paradise of Eden.

Having laid this foundation, let's look at the nature of the role woman was created to play.

## Chapter Two

# The Divine Match

From the first, God created the woman to fulfill the profound need for companionship felt by the man, but not only for this need. She was also brought to life to work side by side with him in the mission given by God. This mission was too important and complex for Adam to accomplish alone. The loneliness he felt was not a loneliness of the soul, because for those who live in full fellowship with God, there is no such loneliness. But Adam could not accomplish the God- given mission by himself.

### Created last, but not least

It is of fundamental importance to understand that the woman had always been part of the original plan of God's creation for his mission on earth, even though she was the last to be created.

No one should think that the creation of the woman was not in the mind of the Creator, and that it was a last minute decision. Make no mistake, without the woman the mission given to Adam could not be fully carried out by him. Beyond that, without her, the specific mission of being fruitful and increasing in number on earth would have been inconceivable.

The woman was created as a helper on the same level of the man, designed and fully able to be co-participant in the integral mission given to both. Since the beginning, in His plan, God designated a ministry for the woman. She was born to accomplish something that was inside the heart of God. To cut off the ministry of the woman is to cut off the DNA planted by God inside of her when she was created.

## Created from Man

The biblical author beautifully describes the marvelous way the woman was created:

*So the LORD God caused the man to fall into a deep sleep; and while he was sleeping, he took one of the man's ribs and closed up the place with flesh. Then the LORD God made a woman from the rib he had taken out of the man, and he brought her to the man* (Gen. 2:21, 22).

The man was created out of the dust of the earth. The woman was created out of the man—from the same substance, the dust of the earth, but out of the man. Because she was formed from Adam, from his bones and flesh, and not directly out of the earth, the woman fulfilled the man as his suitable companion.

## When Adam met Eve

It is important to notice the man's very first revealing conclusion when God brought the first woman to him. When Adam met the woman, he acknowledged her as another being equal to him and from the same species. And he made a poetic declaration as he saw her:

*This is now bone of my bones and flesh of my flesh;*
*she shall be called woman, for she was taken out of*
*man* (Gen. 2:23).

Adam did not find it difficult to call her *woman,* for he recognized that she was completely adequate for him, and that she was his perfect match. More than that, she was part of him — she had been taken out of him.

## The First Love Poem

When the man saw the woman, the first thing he said came out in a poetic format. The first poet was then born. His declaration is a true love poem. As he calls her *ishshah* (woman), Adam creates a word formed out of the word for man — *ish.* He is affirming the relationship, the identification and the interdependence that existed between the two of them.

The term used then shows that he recognized that they were one flesh. "The poetical exclamation of the man, acknowledges the equality of both, concerned to their humanity, what distinguishes them from the other created beings, the animals".[1]

The man's declaration has a highly significant content. The term used for woman defines the identity of this wonderful and unique human being who fulfilled his expectation for companionship. Adam had found no one like her in the whole creation of God. When he contemplated the woman for the first time, his mouth pronounced the strong term *ishshah* (woman), which means *taken out of me* or *formed out of me.* It was a declaration that meant more than a fulfilled necessity. This has great significance, for it was said by the man himself.

It meant that she was the other missing perfect part of him. She was the person he was hoping to find among God's creation. It was a divine encounter. Suddenly, Adam woke up, and his eyes were open to see the reality. He must have considered how he could have lived that long without that woman. It was love at first sight. From that moment on, he realized that he could only go on with his existence, please the Lord, and accomplish the task he had been given if she were with him and if she were part of him. She had been taken out of his side. Back to his side she should return and by his side she should stay forever. For this reason she is indispensable. Among those beings created by God, no one else was so qualified and capable of helping him and fully completing his existence. Not even a talented angel sent from heaven would have had such a powerful effect on the man's existence. God had to create the woman.

## God's Gift to Man

As we see, the process of the creation of the woman was different from the creation of the man, and it was covered with a special mystery and honor. The woman was created out of the man (1 Cor. 11:8), because of him, and to support him in his mission. And to make it special, she was given to the man by God as a gift.

> *Then the LORD God made a woman from the rib he had taken out of the man, and he brought her to the man* (Gen. 2:22).

Since the beginning, the woman was a gift from God to man. She was created by God, had her origin in God, but in an extraordinary way she was born from man. Paul understood it very well. That is probably why he said that "*in the*

*Lord, however, woman is not independent of man, nor is man independent of woman" (I Cor. 11:11).*

They are interdependent for their lives and for their mission. The man, as well as the woman, received from God a ministry to be fulfilled. If the man has a ministry to fulfill, so does the woman. If her ministry is diminished then his ministry is incomplete. If she has no ministry, so he has none either. The interdependency explained by the apostle reveals, in an unquestionable way, the mystery of God's wonderful plan for the ministry of men and women. And that ministry is tied together.

## Chapter Three

# A Joint Mission since Day One

Man and woman received from God a joint mission with similar responsibilities. Eve was given a peculiar function as part of the mission, beyond all the other responsibilities given by God. The biblical account leaves no doubts that the couple received a combined mission:

> *So God created man in his own image, in the image of God he created him; male and female he created them. God blessed them and said to them, "Be fruitful and increase in number; fill the earth and subdue it. Rule over the fish of the sea and the birds of the air and over every living creature that moves on the ground* (Gen. 1:27, 28).

This passage shows that God expected the couple to be fruitful, to multiply and to fill the earth with other human beings. Subduing the earth and the animals was also included in their responsibilities. It is obvious that in order for them to fill the earth with other human beings, Adam and Eve would need each other. To the couple was given dominion over the whole creation (Ps.8: 3-8, Heb.2: 6-8). It is relevant to notice here that the woman also received this dominion. She was qualified to be a suitable helper to the man and to participate with God in His plan to fill the earth and to exert His sovereignty over the whole world.

## A Joint Mission after Calvary

In spite of sin, man and woman were restored to their positions as rulers of the earth with the authority given by God, by the powerful work of Christ in the cross of Calvary (Ps. 8: 4-6). If in the creation they were expected to carry out their missions together, much more now they are expected to do so, since they are now washed in the blood of Christ and filled by the Holy Spirit. Men and women can be trusted with God's authority to advance in their mission.

It is clear from the perspective of the creation and from the cross that women have received a calling from God, have been empowered by the Holy Spirit and have been gifted with talents and spiritual gifts. The work of Christ in the cross has already brought complete salvation and restoration of the mission of men and of women. Acknowledging it releases the grace of Christ and the power of the alliance sealed with His precious blood.

## Woman's Unique Mission

It is unquestionable that woman was specially blessed by God to play a fundamental role in conception and birth. This is her most unique mission to humanity and also to God, because she is the one to conceive God's children into this world to become God's recipients and instruments of His grace to the world. The man did not receive this capacity, though without his participation it would not be possible for the woman to conceive. In this role, as well as in others, woman is the suitable partner for man.

## Woman's Unique Name

When Adam understood this mission of the woman, he called her *Eve*, a noun that means *the mother of all human beings* (Gen. 3:20). This noun defines her unique mission in God's plan of filling the earth. The woman shines in her motherhood mission. The uniqueness of her mission remains fruitful today in every culture, religion, race and nation. The woman has power to bring human beings to life. Only she can do this.

## The Source of Authority

The Scriptures show that authority has a direct relation to the source of creation. This means that one's source of origin has authority over the born being. Christ, the begotten Son of God, submitted Himself to God, establishing through His attitude a pattern for others who were still to be created (Ps.2:7; Col.1:15; Heb.1:5; 5:5). Man, created by God through Christ, is supposed to have Christ as his head and to submit his life to Him (Gen.1:26, 27; Col.1:14-16; Heb.1:3, 10). Woman is supposed to have the man, who is her husband, as her head, and to submit her life to him, because she was created from man (Gen. 2:18-23; 1 Cor. 11:8-9; 1 Tim.2:13). Following the same pattern, children, born from their parents, are supposed to submit to them (Gen.1:28; Eph.6:1, 2; Col.3:20).

Paul explains this relationship of authority in his first letter to the Corinthians (1 Cor. 11), a key passage that we will study in detail in chapter 7. The mission of the woman, as the mother of children, has important implications for her role in church, as she is God's instrument for giving birth to new life. This point will be clarified as we study 1Timothy 2 in chapter 10 of this book.

## Woman's Strategic Ministry

The plan put in action by Satan in the garden did not destroy the strategic plan of God. Immediately after the fall of the first couple, God presented His solution for the problem created by their sin:

*And I will put enmity between you and the woman, and between your offspring and hers; he will crush your head, and you will strike his heel* (Gen. 3:15).

In this prophecy, the Lord declared that from the woman who had been attacked by the poison of the serpent, would be born someone who would be the antidote to destroy the power of the enemy. From this side of History we know that this remedy has already come and is Jesus Christ. The male made no physical contribution to the birth of Christ. Christ was born of woman from the seed of the Holy Spirit. Since the beginning of all things, the Word of God pointed to a day when all things would be restored and controlled again by the hands of men and women in Christ Jesus.

It was through a woman that Satan brought destruction to humanity. But in God's marvelous plan, it was also through a woman that God brought salvation to humanity. That is why the angel Gabriel greeted Mary the way he did when he came to her to foretell the birth of Jesus Christ.

*The angel went to her and said: Greetings, you who are highly favored! The Lord is with you* (Lk. 1:28).

What a greeting to hear! What a word! Mary was receiving a special word sent directly from God's throne about a mission He was entrusting to her. She was highly favored for that. She was being entrusted with Jesus Christ, the very Word of God. The Word who was in the beginning with God, the Word who was God, would become flesh and make His dwelling among men, and let the world see His glory, the glory of the One and Only who would come from the Father, full of grace and truth (John 1:1,14). Since before the creation of the world that mission was determined by God and assigned to a woman. This marvelous mission that would transform all humanity and that would affect all powers in the universe, God entrusted to a woman. A woman carried the Word of God, the exact expression of God's Being in her womb, and gave birth to Him into the world! What a privilege! What an honor! What a grace of God! What a ministry! How can women be forbidden to carry the Word of God, to preach and to teach it to the church and to the world? How would God forbid that?

Mary was highly favored on behalf of all women in Christ. Yes, women have ministries to accomplish for God. Yes, women can carry the Word of God and preach to the whole world. Yes! Yes! Yes! No doubt about that.

May God help the whole church to see with the eyes of the Holy Spirit, the scope and the depth of this marvelous and unspeakable grace of Christ!

## Chapter Four

# The Wonderful
# Order of Creation

God followed an order for creating the world. To understand the order of creation of man and woman is of crucial importance to comprehend the role of women in family, church, and society. Let us review their creation; now focusing on the first steps taken by God when He created man and woman, then we will better understand the sequence of His creation.

## Creation Planned in Heaven

First of all, there was a heavenly summit between God the Father, God the Son, and God the Holy Spirit, and they made a unanimous decision to create man and woman.

*Then God said, "Let us make man in our image, in our likeness, and let them rule over the fish of the sea and the birds of the air, over the livestock, over all the earth, and over all the creatures that move along the ground." So God created man in His own image,*

*in the image of God He created him; male and female
He created them* (Gen.1: 26, 27).

The Trinity's decision to create "them," as the verse
reads, was accomplished in the sixth day. Both man and
woman were created in the image of God, which distin-
guished them from the other creatures. In spite of the fact
that the Scriptures are clear about this, there are some theological controversies that surround it. They are not about the
order of creation itself or about the definitions of the roles
designated by God in the beginning. But they refer to the
interpretations and implications of theological and cultural
patterns mistakenly adopted by the church, such as "to attri-
bute to man a superior status over woman, or to argue that
he was created in the image of God while the woman was
created in the image of man, being therefore only a reflected
image of God, a kind of second level of creation." [2]

All arguments that disregard women fall flat if we understand, through the Scriptures, that she too was created in the
image of God. This is clearly stated in Genesis 1: 27.

## Understanding God's Poetry

In Genesis 1:27 we have the first occurrence of poetry in
the Old Testament.[3] God is the author of this beautiful and
meaningful poem. Hebrew poetry uses parallelism. Ideas and
thoughts are combined to create a peculiar type of repetition. In synonymic parallelism[4], poetry is arranged in such a
way that some phrases or lines are repeated in the following
lines to expand the idea and to reinforce the meaning of the
stanza. The thought or idea is emphasized, even though it
may sound redundant. In this poem, the verse was poetically
structured on this form:

1st line: God created man in His own image,
2nd line: in the image of God He created him;
3rd line: male and female He created them.

The poetic author of Genesis confirms and concludes in the third line the thoughts and truths affirmed in the first and second lines, and that truth is man and woman were created in the image of God.

This passage uses a figure of speech called "anadiplosis".[5] This figure repeats the final word (words or synonymous words) of one phrase or clause at the beginning of the next clause. In this verse, the first and the second lines safely establish that man was created in the image of God. Note the composition of the idea being said repeatedly in the underlined words:

"So God created man <u>in His image,</u>
<u>In the image of God</u> He created him;

So, the first composition equates "in His image" (first line) to "in the image of God" (second line). The meaning is: man was created in the image of God.

The second and the third lines present another composition. The reference to the man at the end of the second line includes the woman, and is explained in the repetition at the beginning of the third line. Again, note the underlined words:

"In the image of God He created <u>him;</u>
<u>Male and female</u> He created them."

This composition equates "him" (man) to "male and female" (man and woman). The meaning is: God created man and woman in His image. As Araujo Filho says clearly and poetically in his commentary on this verse, "The image of God is present in the woman the same way it is in the man. Man and woman have the same capacity to perceive God, to understand their need for holiness, to reflect about the divinity of God, about their moral feelings and their inherent dignity. The image of God places man and woman on the same podium of creation, at the same level and with the same ability to share equivalent perceptions."[6] And I add equivalent mission and ministry. In order to leave no doubt about this truth, the Word of God repeats the concept in Genesis 5: 1, 2:

> *"When God created man, he made him in the likeness of God. He created them male and female and blessed them. And when they were created, he called them "man."*

God called both of them Adam, as a single unit created in His image.

### God Created Adam First

After having planted a garden in Eden, God formed the first man from the dust of the earth.

> *The Lord God formed the man from the dust of the ground and breathed into his nostrils the breath of life, and the man became a living being* (Gen. 2: 7).

God put the man in the Garden of Eden to cultivate and guard it. He gave clear commandments to him, determined his tasks in the garden, and oriented him to choose the way of life (Gen. 2:15-17).

## Then God Created Eve

*So the Lord God caused the man to fall into a deep*
*sleep; and while he was sleeping, He took one of the*
*man's ribs and closed up the place with flesh. Then*
*the Lord God made a woman from the rib He had*
*taken out of the man, and He brought her to man*
(Gen. 2:21, 22).

God formed the woman from a man's rib and made him a
surprise. He gave her to him as a gift. This act of God means
that the wife is a gift from God to her husband. In this way,
God established marriage and family.

## The Order of Creation as Paul's Theological Basis

At this point in our biblical construct, it is appropriate
to demonstrate how the apostle Paul understands the order
of creation and how he uses it as a theological basis for his
instructions about the position of man and woman in family
and in church. Paul's instruction to the church of Corinth has
as its central point the order of creation:

*Now I want you to realize that the head of every man*
*is Christ, and the head of the woman is man, and the*
*head of Christ is God.* (1 Cor. 11:3).

The spiritual relationship described by Paul reveals an
order of spiritual authority based on the order of creation that
includes and gives prominence to the person of Jesus Christ.
The ultimate purpose for the order of authority is to exalt the
person of Jesus Christ as Lord.

The connection – Christ – man — woman, so beautiful
and so unique, is granted only to men and women among
all created beings. It carries profound implications for their

relationship with God and with their spouses, and for their functions and ministries in church. The greater purpose of anything in life and of any relationship, especially in family and in ministry, is that Christ receives the glory and honor.

## The Order of Creation Determines the Order of Authority

In 1 Corinthians 11, the Greek word translated as "head" (v. 3) is *kephale,* and it may mean either "head" or "chief."[7] Paul reveals that there is an order of authority to be respected in the Kingdom of God: as Christ is the head, the spiritual chief of man, so is the man the spiritual authority of his wife.

Paul explains the order of authority. "For man did not come from woman, but woman from man" (v.8), and also "neither was man created for woman, but woman for man" (v.9). This order was established by God to maintain the relational ecology between the couple and all of humanity to come.

When instructing his disciple Timothy, pastor of the church of Ephesus, about women in church, Paul gives the same reason for his instruction: "*...for Adam was formed first, then Eve*" (1 Tim. 2:13). Paul focused on the authority in the family, which should respect the order of creation, for man was created first, and not woman, and woman for man and not otherwise. The history of creation cannot be changed. It was so in the beginning. It was the same in Paul's time. And it is certainly still valid for today: Adam was formed first, then Eve. The order of creation cannot be changed. Neither can the order of authority. The order of creation explains and establishes the order of authority.

## Just a Matter of Order

In order to better clarify this point, let us consider the children of a couple. The parents are the authority over them because of the order of creation. But it does not mean that they are inferior to their parents; they merely came to life after them. They were entrusted to their parents by God. The children are created by God, have their origin in God, even though they were born from their parents. Children have to honor and to obey their parents, for this attitude pleases the Lord (Col.3:20). And why does it please the Lord? Because they are learning how to be submissive to God as they are submissive to their parents. In this apprenticeship their hearts are being transformed from a rebellious inclination to a submissive one, in preparation to obey the Lord. They are learning submission.

Therefore, the woman was not created as inferior to man for having been created later. She was simply created *after* him. It is just a matter of order. Authority is given to man as a mission and submission is required from woman as part of her co-mission. Her submission pleases God because she is learning how to be submissive to Him as she walks in submission to her husband. In this apprenticeship, the natural rebellious inclination of her heart is being replaced by a submissive one. She is learning submission.

The single women and men are in the same situation. As children, they must walk under the authority of their parents (Eph. 6:2). Home is the first place where they should learn the submission that pleases the Lord. In the same way, the married woman will learn in the school of submission with her husband.

Likewise, men are also subjected to the same command-ment to learn to walk in submission. They have to walk in submission to Jesus, who is the Head of every man. They have to learn submission to Jesus and to his wife. A man learns submission to Christ as he learns how to lead their families under Christ's headship. He learns submission to his wife as he learns how to serve and take care of her as Christ does to His church. He submits to her need, and she submits to his lead. That is how they submit to one another. That submission pleases their Lord Jesus Christ.

If he is a Christian, he is commanded to walk in submission in the church. According to Paul, walking in submission to one another in the church is a natural result of lives filled with the Holy Spirit. Only Spirit-filled men and women can walk in submission out of their reverence to their Lord Jesus Christ.

*Instead, be filled with the Spirit. Speak to one another with psalms, hymns and spiritual songs. Sing and make music in your heart to the Lord, always giving thanks to God the Father for everything, in the name of our Lord Jesus Christ. Submit to one another out of reverence for Christ* (Eph. 5:18-21).

### Learning from Eve's Failure

When Eve left her spiritual position of walking in submission and accountability to Adam, she was soon deceived by the serpent. She gave Satan a foothold and fell into sin. It is necessary to admit that Eve was the one initially deceived by Satan (1 Tim. 2:14). This shows that the human nature seems to be vulnerable to Satan's deceptions in the absence of submission and accountability. In other words, all human beings, including single women, single men, married women, and married men, need to learn and to practice spiritual submission and accountability to gain protection from the devil's schemes. Unfortunately, in Eden, the woman was the first one to leave the safe order of submission. She was then followed by Adam.

The relationships, first with the parents and later with her spouse, are the woman's primary ministries. If she operates well in her home, her new Garden of Eden, she will do well in the church. If she demonstrates she is a good learner and practitioner of submission and accountability to those who are her spiritual authorities, she will prove her heart is in tune with the Lord and will be able to walk in submission to Him. This attitude will qualify her to minister in the church. The first laboratory to test the ministry of the woman is her home.

## The Non-negotiable Requirement for Man

Man also has to go through a test before ministering in the church. Note Paul's instructions for those who desire to serve the Lord in church leadership:

*If anyone sets his heart on being an overseer, he desires a noble task. Now the overseer…must manage his own family well and see that his children obey him with proper respect* (1 Tim. 3:1-5).

This passage states clearly that man should first be trained at home in how to govern his family and raise obedient children, if he will to be considered qualified to carry out ministry in church. The kind of authority he is supposed to practice is of a spiritual order and has to present some visible results in his family life, which are described in the same passage. In other words, his home is also his primary ministry place. If he demonstrates that he is able to govern his house according to the model the Scriptures determine, he will be considered qualified to minister in the church. In other words, the picture of a man's wife and their children will show crystal clearly if he is qualified to minister to the church of God. This condition is nonnegotiable.

## A Law of Life for All

In summary, God created man and woman in His own image and likeness and followed an order through which spiritual authority was established. This order is a law of life for all, both Christians and non-Christians. All who obey it will be blessed, because it is a path of life determined by God in Creation.

## Chapter Five

# Ecological Disaster in Eden

Everything was going well in Eden. There was a real and complete harmony until a very sinister and astute being appeared with the determined purpose of provoking an ecological disaster in that perfect ecology of relationships.

*Now the serpent was craftier than any of the wild animals the LORD God had made. He said to the woman, "Did God really say, `You must not eat from any tree in the garden'?" The woman said to the serpent, "We may eat fruit from the trees in the garden, but God did say, `You must not eat fruit from the tree that is in the middle of the garden, and you must not touch it, or you will die.'" "You will not surely die," the serpent said to the woman. "For God knows that when you eat of it your eyes will be opened, and you will be like God, knowing good and evil." When the woman saw that the fruit of the tree was good for food and pleasing to the eye, and also desirable for gaining wisdom, she took some and ate it. She also gave some to her husband, who was with her, and he ate it. Then the eyes of both of them were* *opened, and they realized they were naked; so they sewed fig leaves together and made coverings for themselves* (Gen. 3:1-7).

The woman was deceived and unfortunately missed the opportunity to keep accountability in her relationship to her husband, and so brought fatal consequences to all future humanity. She had received from God the capacity to cooperate and to complete the mission given to Adam. She had been created as a suitable helper, not as his leader. The episode in the Garden of Eden demonstrated that she was not competent to exert the leadership of the couple. She made an isolated decision. She had not been created to walk alone, and she did not discern that her decision could have strong spiritual repercussions and that it was not simply about choosing the dessert for dinner.

It was a spiritual decision that interfered in the relationship of the couple with God and affected God's purpose for them, as well as the future of their lives and of their descendents. Eve either confused or forgot her role in the mission for which she had been created. The error was fatal. It provoked a disaster in the relational ecology that was beautifully operating in the garden.

## An Open Gate in Eden

Eve's sinful desire to eat the prohibited fruit worked against her. Her desire opened the door to sin, and Satan entered through it immediately after having discovered the weaknesses in the relationship of the first couple. Later we see the same thing happening to their son, Cain. He wanted to kill his brother, Abel, and God alerted him by saying *"If you do not do what is right, sin is crouching at your door; it desires to have you, but you must master it"* (Gen. 4:7).

There are other biblical examples we can learn from, such as the episode of Jezebel and Ahab. She reigned over Israel and dominated her husband, King Ahab, with serious consequences to the nation. Mary, mother of Jesus Christ, at the wedding at Cana in Galilee, misused her position as the earthly mother of Jesus, when she wanted him to reveal himself to the world ahead of time. Jesus said to her: *"Dear woman, why do you involve me? My time has not yet come"* (John 2: 4). On another occasion, Mary, with her other children, sought for Jesus in order to get him and to take charge of him, thinking that he was out of his mind (Mk. 3:20-21; 31- 35). Her emotions took over and prevented her from having spiritual discernment about her role in Jesus' life.

What happened in the Garden of Eden demonstrated also that Adam was not competent in his role as the leader of the couple. He paid more attention to the woman's voice than to God's. He had to be accountable to God for the couple's decisions. Adam followed his heart and disobeyed God's commandment. He was the one who had heard the commandment directly from God. He was expected to help Eve to understand it and to be obedient to it. But because he did not do that, God held him responsible for the disobedience and for its consequences (Rom. 5:12).

## An Ecological Disaster in the Ecology of Relationships

The weaknesses of man and woman were discovered and exploited by Satan. The woman's weakness was shown in Eve's attitude. She confessed to God that she disobeyed His commandment because the serpent had deceived her.

*Then the LORD God said to the woman, "What is this you have done?" The woman said, "The serpent deceived me, and I ate." (Gen.3.13).*

Later, the apostle Paul confirms it:

*And Adam was not the one deceived; it was the woman who was deceived and became a sinner* (1 Tim. 2:14).

## Consequences for the Woman

In the Garden of Eden the woman heard a direct judgment from God, which affected her specifically in her peculiar mission of giving birth. A mission that was originally planned to be a pleasure to her, from that point on would become difficult and painful (Gen. 3: 16a).

Concerning her relationship to her husband, a significant change would occur as a consequence of her sin. The sentence of the Creator included a second part: "Your desire will be for your husband, and he will rule over you" (Gen. 3: 16b). A relationship that so far had followed easily and harmoniously in accountability to each other, from that point on, would face new challenges. It would not be as easy as it used to be. The harmony of the relationship would depend much more on her than on her husband, for she would have to learn how to submit to his governance.

At first glance it may seem to be a hard sentence to accept and to understand, but the grace of God can clearly be seen in it. By establishing this new rule for the couple's relationship, God put in operation a safeguard against possible new attacks of Satan against Eve and all women born after her. Discipline enters in as an aspect of this new rule, which needs to be clearly understood for the good of their relationship and their common mission. This discipline does not mean that the woman can not desire anything else in life. It means that she needs to hear from God, that she should submit her decisions to her husband and be sure to be accountable to him.

If, instead of deciding by herself, Eve had asked the serpent to excuse her for five minutes to ask for her husband's opinion about what she was being tempted to do, Satan would have failed in that attack against humanity. The couple had never eaten that fruit before, and more than that, it was prohibited. And Eve knew it. It was her duty to consult with Adam, since God had entrusted the mission on earth to the couple, not to her alone.

By making her independent decision, Eve was disrespectful of Adam and of God. She disregarded him as her companion and disregarded the consequences that decision would bring to their lives and to humanity. Eve failed humanity. Had she taken those five minutes she could have avoided much trouble for all creation.

## Consequences for the Man

Adam became indebted to Eve and to humanity when he failed to exert the role of a responsible man before God concerning the commandment he had received from his Creator. He failed to guard God's commandment, to guard Eve and to guard the garden. Why would a garden need a guard? The garden had to be guarded from something, which is why God had put him there as His special guard. One of Adam's tasks was to guard the garden from the evil one.

The relationship between the man and the soil was also harmed. As part of the sentence for that act of disobedience, the soil was cursed, and from that time on, the man would have to face new enemies, thorns, and thistles. The man's work of cultivating the soil to get food for his survival would become more difficult (Gen. 3:17b).

God revealed to Adam a terrible consequence for his sin: judgment would come upon him because he had listened to the woman and had eaten from the tree God had commanded not to eat (Gen. 3:17a). Adam did not listen to God, but to the woman instead. The helper could be listened to, but neither before nor instead of God—and never contrary to God.

In other words, Adam did not listen to God, but disobeyed Him, and indirectly through the woman, he listened to Satan and obeyed him. That was serious and dangerous. Soon Satan discovered that there were footholds in the man's hearts—an inclination to listen to the woman more than he should and to not to watch over her against Satan's attacks. He also found out that the woman had footholds in her heart—an inclination to make decisions alone and an inclination to persuade man. Satan entered through these footholds and took man and woman captive into sin. His first aim was to strike God, and to do so he struck man. Sadly, the means he used to achieve his goal was the woman.

## Ecology of Enmity

From that point on, enmity was brought to the environment of natural life on earth: enmity between man and God; between man and the soil; between man and woman; between woman (with the humanity represented by her) and the serpent. That perfect ecology operating in the Garden of Eden was dramatically broken when another being came into that scene; a being that was not part of the ecosystem of the garden, Satan. Sadly, it was Eve who opened the gate for him. Unfortunately, Adam was not watching it.

## Chapter Six

# God's Rescue Operation

Part of God's gracious solution to restore the ecology of relationships between Him and humanity was extraordinarily revealed through His decision to banish Adam and Eve from the Garden of Eden after the Fall. By doing so, He protected them from eating the fruit of the tree of life. If they ate from that tree, they would become eternally sinners (Gen. 3: 22-25). Therefore, the banishment that came upon them as an act of judgment was also an act of God's marvelous grace for all humanity.

## God's Gracious Salvation Plan

But God had salvation prepared for them through the coming of the one who would be born from woman—Jesus Christ—as man, in order to save from death all those who would believe in Him. The Lord Jesus Christ, the Savior who had been chosen since before the foundation of the world, would descend from woman and would defeat the serpent:

*And I will put enmity between you and the woman, and between your offspring and hers; he will crush your head, and you will strike his heel* (Gen. 3: 15).

Eternal life would be given to those who believed in Him (Rom.5:12, 17-19). Far from Eden and from the tree of life, God's plan for the salvation of humanity would unfold with the coming of the Savior to earth.

## God's Gracious Discipline for Woman

Likewise, God's sentence for the woman—"*your desire will be to your husband, and he will rule over you*" (Gen. 3:16b)—includes the grace and wisdom of God to humanity, as well as a strategic and secret defense mechanism against future attempts of Satan to attack and harm the relationship between man and woman.

At first glance, it is difficult to understand, but if we pay close attention we can hear the grace of God in that declaration to Eve. As it was a spiritual pronouncement, it can only be spiritually discerned. This divine decision works as a shield to protect the woman from the enemy, who will not give up his attacks, always generating deceit and error within the human race.

Man was given the responsibility to walk alongside his wife and help her to discern God's will and make the right decisions. They are supposed to walk in accountability to each other, but the responsibility for the couple's decisions lies on the man's shoulders. The woman needs to accept this as a gracious and just act of God in her favor, a security precaution divinely activated for her own good and for the good of the family.

## What was changed in the Woman-man Relationship?

The relationship between man and woman now has an element of discipline. But that discipline overflows with the grace and love of God. If it is received and practiced in love and accountability, it will lock the door to Satan, preventing his attempts to infiltrate their marriage and family relationships.

Even today, Satan tries to deceive women and men, regarding that divine decision. Many men insist that women were placed by God in an inferior position of subservience to men, because of the deceit of Eve. In fact, this has been the interpretation and attitude of many people and races towards women, which has brought all kinds of discrimination, hostility, and enmity between men and women. Especially in cultures where people are under the greatest spiritual errors, women suffer in almost unbearable oppressive and demonic conditions. We can observe this situation in countries where religions such as Buddhism, Islam and others rule over people, and in tribal groups which live under the dominion of voodoo and witchcraft.

Many women seem also to have accepted the idea that they are somehow inferior to men. This position has brought much confusion inside and outside the church, a fact that certainly pleases Satan. Diverse movements have started all around the world with the intention to set women free from this yoke. The intention is healthy, but much prudence is necessary in evaluating such movements. This is because some of them, even in Christian circles, have only an appearance of wisdom and of justice, without godliness.

Any kind of error or deceit which provokes injustice and oppression can only be solved or eliminated by the light of truth found in the Word of God: "Then you will know the truth, and the truth will set you free" (John. 8:32). Truth must be women's justice and instrument of liberation.

### What Jesus did for the Church He did for Women

The God of all wisdom and knowledge, who is full of grace, mercy, and love, does love women as intensely as He loves men. His love reached out to Adam, as well as to Eve. The sacrifice of Jesus was sufficient to erase the sins of men and of women, as the author of the Hebrew letter clarifies:

*And by that will, we have been made holy through the sacrifice of the body of Jesus Christ once for all* (Heb.10.10).

In the context of the tenth chapter of Hebrews, this means that Jesus Christ has erased the memory of the sin of Adam and also of Eve.

According to the apostle Paul, Adam was considered by God to be responsible for the entrance of sin and death into the world (Rom. 5:12). Jesus Christ, the last Adam, therefore closed the door to sin and to death, and opened a door to justification and to eternal life (Rom. 5:17-18). Christ came to confirm the covering pre-figured in Eden when God made garments of skin to cloth Adam and Eve (Gen. 3: 21). Paul explains this mystery:

*You are all sons of God through faith in Christ Jesus, for all of you who were baptized into Christ have clothed yourselves with Christ. There is neither Jew nor Greek, slave nor free, male nor female, for you are all one in Christ Jesus* (Gal. 3:26-28).

That spiritual covering in Christ includes all, who according to the Law, were kept apart from God and from all other human beings. All are united in the Body of Christ where there is no Greek, Jew, slave, free, man, or woman. In the Body of Christ there are no distinctions or divisions. On the contrary, the functions are planned with the purpose of promoting unity. All have their positions and spaces secured in the Body. All are spiritual stones of the building God is constructing for His own habitation (1 Pet. 2:4-5).

The understanding Paul had about this subject is once more expressed in an unquestioning way as he said:

*So from now on we regard no one from a worldly point of view. Though we once regarded Christ in this way, we do so no longer. Therefore, if anyone is in Christ, he is a new creation; the old has gone, the new has come!* (2 Cor. 5:16-17).

In this profound declaration Paul reveals that he saw the functions of his brothers and sisters in Christ through the Spirit. He did not look at them with the eyes of his natural understanding. He saw them as members of God's family and citizens of His Kingdom (Eph. 2:19).

In other words, new life in Christ brings a new vision of the members of His body. All who put their faith in Christ belong to a spiritual body whose head is Jesus Christ. Some are eyes; others are feet, hands, ligaments or ears, well adjusted to edify the Body of Christ (Eph. 4:11-16; 1 Cor. 12:12-31).

Paul would look at a converted Jew, still linked to the Jewish traditions, and see him within the Body of Christ as an eye or a pastor perhaps. Paul would look at a saved gentile who could still feel like a stranger in the church and see him in the Body of Christ as a foot or an evangelist. He would look at a woman, usually despised by the culture, and see her in the Body of Christ as an arm or a teacher.

I believe that Paul took deep joy in the revelation of the mystery of the church and in the destruction of the oppressive, political, cultural and demonic powers that building up the church provoked. In his letter to the Ephesians, he expresses his joy in passing on to the church the revelation he had the privilege of receiving from God.

*For this reason I, Paul, the prisoner of Christ Jesus for the sake of you Gentiles— Surely you have heard about the administration of God's grace that was given to me for you, that is, the mystery made known to me by revelation, as I have already written briefly. In reading this, then, you will be able to understand my insight into the mystery of Christ, which was not made known to men in other generations as it has now been revealed by the Spirit to God's holy apostles and prophets. This mystery is that through the gospel the Gentiles are heirs together with Israel, members together of one body, and sharers together in the promise in Christ Jesus. I became a servant of this gospel by the gift of God's grace given me through the working of his power. Although I am less than the least of all God's people, this grace was given me: to preach to the Gentiles the unsearchable riches of Christ, and to make plain to everyone the administration of this mystery, which for ages past was kept hidden in God, who created all things. His intent was that now, through the church, the manifold wisdom of God should be made known to the rulers and authorities in the heavenly realms, and according to his eternal purpose which he accomplished in Christ Jesus our Lord. In him and through faith in him we may approach God with freedom and confidence* (Eph. 3:1-12).

In this same letter Paul prays twice asking God to give his readers a spirit of wisdom and of revelation, so that all together, they could comprehend the mystery of the church, so that the glory of Christ could be manifested through the church (Eph. 1:15-23; 3:15-21). In the letter to the Christians of Ephesus he clearly states that only when all find their places in the Body of Christ and are acknowledged as such, will the glory of Christ be manifested through His church (Eph. 3: 8-10, 21).

This is equivalent to saying that Jews, gentiles, men, and women, when integrated into the Body of Christ, have their natural characteristics according to the flesh absorbed into a spiritual body, in which new spiritual characteristics will be developed. Certainly a Jew continues to be Jew, a European continues to be European, a man continues to be man, and a woman is still woman. But the Body of Christ, the "mature man," as a supra gender, supra cultural and supra racial spiritual organism, sets aside the earthly point of view to take its position as "seated in the heavenly realm in Christ Jesus" (Eph. 2:6), and receives a new understanding about its own nature, identity, mission, and membership. It is of crucial importance to be able to comprehend in depth the Pauline revelation about the church overall explained in the letter to the Ephesians. Only then can we fully understand who we are as men and women in this spiritual Body of Christ.

When this understanding is achieved, the biblical passages that refer particularly to women which are considered by many to be "controversial," will not be threatening weapons any more to the female members of the Body of Christ. It is past time for women to be afraid and oppressed. Satan was defeated, and men and women are free to work, united and peacefully, in the church. They are members of the same Body of Christ; they are one in Christ.

Powerful learning is to be drawn from the fact that the woman is a figure of the church in the New Testament. We will see later in this book (chapter 11) that the church, which is supposed to walk in submission to her Head Jesus Christ, has a commandment to preach the Gospel, teach the Word of God, and manifest His power to all world. As the church is not constrained or limited by any spiritual or governmental power to do her ministry in the world, so is the woman not limited. If the church has ministry, so has the woman. To imply that a woman cannot speak or teach God's Word to the world, is the same as suggesting that the church should be silent in the world.

In the second part of this book we will investigate the main New Testament passages and come to a harmonious and sound position about the ministry of women, with implications for the ministry of the whole church.

# PART TWO

# DISCLOSING THE SECRET
# BEHIND THE VEIL

Christian women in Corinth wore a veil in contrast to women who ministered in the pagan temples in the city. Paul borrowed from the cultural context the figure of the veil and used it in 1 Corinthians chapter 11 as a metaphor to express a spiritual principle that has powerful effects in a woman's life. Unfortunately, the veil has been misunderstood and misused.

Behind the metaphor of the veil there is a spiritual secret about the position of a woman in the family which explains her role in the church and in society. This secret will be "unveiled" as we investigate the teachings of the apostle.

The metaphor of the veil teaches us that a woman needs a spiritual covering to be authorized to minister. If she wears this spiritual covering, she will gain her husband's respect and she will not have problems with her children's submission. She will be released to minister to the Body of Christ. Her position of spiritual dominion in the heavenly realms will be recovered in Christ Jesus. Spiritually dressed like that, she will be qualified to fight the good fight she is called to win for God and with God. Covered with this spiritual veil, nobody can stop her ministry. Not even Satan. This is because Jesus Christ authorizes her to minister, and His authority is incontestable everywhere, especially in His church.

# Chapter Seven

# The Veil of the Woman
## 1 Corinthians 11: 2-16

To better understand the teachings of Paul to the Church of Jesus Christ, let's take a look at some cultural, social and religious aspects of the city of Corinth at the time the first letter to the Corinthians was written.

### The Religious Environment of Corinth

When Paul lived in the cosmopolitan Greek city of Corinth, approximately 250,000 free people and 400,000 slaves made their homes there. He stayed in Corinth for 18 months, probably between the years 50 and 52 A.D. (Acts 1:8).

The Corinthians were pagans interested in human wisdom, Greek philosophy, and religion. There were at least twelve pagan temples in the city. Among the false gods worshipped in the city were Aphrodite, Cybele, Apollo and Asclepius. Aphrodite was the goddess of love, and in her temple, physical love was exalted and approximately one thousand temple prostitutes ministered there. Cybele, the goddess of nature and wild animals, received her worshippers in wild and orgiastic feasts. Apollo was the god of sunlight, prophecy, music, and poetry, and Asclepius, the god of healing.

Corinth was well known by the liberal practice of prostitution. The immorality and the promiscuity of the city were so largely known that the verb *korinthiazein* (to corinthianize) came to mean "to practice sexual immorality and to live in promiscuity."[8] Some temples were controlled by priestesses who committed sexual acts with the attendees as a form of worship. They wore distinctive outfits and shaved their heads.

It was in this religious environment that Paul preached the Gospel. He started preaching in a Jewish synagogue but was not welcomed by the Jews and decided to preach to the Gentiles. That was the beginning of the Church at Corinth. Later on, Paul left the city and went to Ephesus, and while at Ephesus members of the household of Chloe brought him a report about the Corinthian Church, now facing many problems. Paul wrote his first letter to the Church to correct some errors and to give instructions.

## A Fresh Look of 1 Corinthians 11

To begin let us restate that Paul used the veil to speak about a spiritual principle, not a practice for the Church. He begins the chapter by praising the Church of Corinth for keeping his teachings. Then he offers instruction related to the ministry of men and women in the Church. He states that men and women are free to pray and to prophesy. It is clear that prophetic and intercessory ministries were performed with freedom by men and women in the Corinthian Church.

Paul wants to make sure that these ministries are performed under the right conditions and for the edification of the Church, especially taking into consideration the city where they were serving the Lord. Dishonor to the name of

Jesus had to be avoided at all cost. The Corinthian Christians had to be aware of the religious context of the city and of the spiritual warfare in which they were engaged.

Christian women ministering in the Church should not be mistaken for the priestesses who controlled the pagan temples. The long hair and/or use of the veil was a distinctive and external sign that Christians were not part of the dominant immorality operating in that city, and that they belonged to Jesus Christ.

## A Powerful Connection

In his instruction, Paul reaffirms a principle of spiritual authority which was established according to the order of creation. We already know that the order of creation is the basis for Paul's thinking, especially when it refers to men and women. It was necessary to safeguard their Christian testimonies because of the cultural context in which they lived. The Corinthian society recognized Christian women by the external sign of long hair or of a covering for their heads, the veil.

*Now I want you to realize that the head of every man is Christ, and the head of the woman is man, and the head of Christ is God (1 Cor. 11:3).*

**GOD**
⇓
**CHRIST**
⇓
**MAN**
⇓
**WOMAN**

GOD – CHRIST – MAN – WOMAN – this is the beautiful chain of command through which the apostle describes how the principle of authority operates in God's kingdom. God is the head of Jesus. Christ is the head of all men. An individual man is the head of an individual woman. He is not the head of every woman, but of his wife. It is important to remember that in the Garden of Eden, God gave Eve to Adam to be his wife and they became one flesh:

*For this reason a man will leave his father and mother and be united to his wife, and they will become one flesh* (Gen. 2:24).

Man is the head of this new unit and woman is the body in the extraordinary analogy used by the Apostle Paul (Eph. 5:23). Man **becomes** the head of his woman **only** when he leaves his father and mother and is united in one flesh with her. Woman **becomes** the body of the new unit in the same way.

Understand that Paul is not telling the Church of Corinth that every man in the Church should be head over all the women in the Church. Remember that according to God, a man can only become a head over a woman when he becomes her husband and both become one. But Paul is confirming the order of creation established by God that husbands are the heads of their own wives.

### The Principle of Spiritual Authority in Moses' Law

There is a relevant text in Moses' Law which explains the principle of spiritual authority that Paul was teaching to the Corinthian Church. As a brilliant Old Testament scholar, Paul knew the Law very well and may have had Numbers 30 in mind while he was writing the letter to the Corinthians.

## Concerning Men

Moses wrote God's statute starting with instructions to men:

*When a man makes a vow to the Lord or takes an oath to obligate himself by a pledge, he must not break his word but must do everything he said* (Num. 30:2).

Every man who wanted to make a vow to dedicate himself to God, through the Nazarite vow or any other type of consecration, should understand that he would be obligated to keep his vow until it was fulfilled. There were no mediators between him and God. His responsibility was personal and very serious. He was directly accountable to God. The principle pre-figured in the Law was that Christ is the head of every man.

## Concerning Women

The Law presented a substantial difference concerning women.

### On Single Women

*When a young woman still living in her father's house makes a vow to the Lord or obligates herself by a pledge and her father hears about her vow or pledge but says nothing to her, then all her vows and every pledge by which she obligated herself will stand. But if her father forbids her when he hears about it, none of her vows or pledges by which she obligated herself will stand; the Lord will release her because her father has forbidden her* (Num. 30: 3-5).

The single woman was accountable to God through her father. Every consecration of her life to God had to be approved and authorized by her father. God would forgive her for not keeping her vow if her father was opposed to her desire. If he approved, she was obligated to fulfill her vow to God. This demonstrates that while she remained single in her father's house, he had spiritual authority over her. She was supposed to learn how to walk in submission to that authority. Her father was accountable directly to God for his daughter's spiritual decisions. The principle pre-figured in the Law is that women need spiritual covering.

## On Married Women

*If she marries after she makes a vow or after her lips utter a rash promise by which she obligates herself and her husband hears about it but says nothing to her, then her vows or the pledges by which she obligated herself will stand. But if her husband forbids her when he hears about it, he nullifies the vow that obligates her or the rash promise by which she obligates herself, and the Lord will release her* (Num. 30: 6-8).

*If a woman living with her husband makes a vow or obligates herself by a pledge under oath and her husband hears about it but says nothing to her and does not forbid her, then all her vows or the pledges by which she obligated herself will stand. But if her husband nullifies them when he hears about them, none of the vows or pledges that came from her lips will stand. Her husband has nullified them, and the Lord will release her. Her husband may confirm or nullify any vow she makes or any sworn pledge to deny herself. But if her husband says nothing to her*

*about it from day to day, then he confirms all her*
*vows or the pledges binding on her. He confirms*
*them by saying nothing to her when he hears about*
*them. If, however, he nullifies them some time after*
*he hears about them, then he is responsible for her*
*guilt* (Num. 30:10-15).

When a woman married, the spiritual authority was transferred from her father to her husband. When they become
one flesh, the husband becomes the spiritual authority of the
woman –but only when they marry and become one flesh.
The husband then becomes directly accountable to God for
his wife's spiritual life.

The principle pre-figured in the Law was that a married
woman has a head, and that is her husband. The understanding of this principle is of fundamental importance for
the understating of the women's mission and ministry.

## On Orphan, Divorced and Widowed Women

What was the condition of the divorced, widowed, and
orphaned women, young or old? Here is how the Law dealt
with these cases:

*Any vow or obligation taken by a widowed or divorced*
*woman will be binding on her* (Num. 30:9).

In contrast to single and married women, this verse says
that they were responsible for their own decisions before
God. Why is that so? We have to understand this instruction
in the light of the spiritual principle hidden in it. According
to the principle of the Law we are examining, if widowed
and divorced women walked in submission to their husbands
while they were married, their vows to consecrate their lives
to God were valid. They were valid because they had learned

the lesson of submission in their husband's house in the first place.

The same was true for orphaned single women. If they had learned to submit to their fathers when they were still alive, these women were free to consecrate themselves to ministry after their fathers' deaths. They attended the school of submission at their father's house while they had the opportunity and so were approved.

The Scriptures say that God protects orphans and widows who walk in submission:

> *A father to the fatherless, a defender of widows, is God in His holy dwelling. God sets the lonely in families, He leads forth the prisoners with singing; but the rebellious live in a sun-scorched land* (Ps. 68: 5).

The Law and the Prophets also required that the rich families allowed for orphans and widows to glean on their fields. That was the Law's provision for their support (Deut.14:29; 16:11-14; 24:19-21; Is. 10:2; Jer: 7:6; Zach. 7:10; Mal. 3:5). So, we can conclude that the Law safeguarded those women's rights to be directly accountable to God about their decisions, if they had submissive hearts.

## A Continual Principle in the Law

The text in Numbers 30 sets the relationship between a father and his daughter and a husband and his wife in spiritual matters. The same principle is supported by other biblical passages, which we will analyze further. The repeated principle is: a woman has a spiritual authority over her life. When single, her father is that authority. When married, her husband is her head. This is the order that comes from God's throne of grace for a woman's protection. Have in mind that the woman is also a figure of the Church, which can do nothing without her Head, Jesus Christ (John 15: 5b).

It is obvious that with these instructions God had in mind for fathers and husbands to be faithful spiritual guardians of their daughters and wives. In order to do so, they would have to learn how to listen to God, and how to walk in submission to God's voice. If they misunderstand God's will for the women under them, they would have to bear their guilt before God.

## New Testament Teachings

The Apostle Paul understood this principle very well and built his instruction to the Church of Corinth on this basis. He states that there is a spiritual authority which comes from heaven. It flows from God to Jesus, from Jesus to man, and from man to his wife – within the one flesh unit (vs.3). Everyone included in this order of things is ultimately under God's authority.

## The Special Position of Woman

Woman is the only one who is not called "head." She is called "the glory of man." She has a privileged position of respect and protection. She is cared for during her whole life by her father, by her husband, and by her Lord and Savior, as if she were the apple of his eyes. She was placed in a special position by God. By being the glory of man, she glorifies Jesus, the ultimate honor for which she was created.

The woman has a position of dignity and her spiritual authority has been restored. This is the meaning of Paul's declaration:

*For this reason, and because of the angels, the woman ought to have a sign of authority on her head* (1 Cor. 11:10).

Her spiritual authority is restored before the angels. Paul declares to the Ephesians that the Church makes the multiform wisdom of God known to the powers and principalities in the heavenly places (Eph. 3:10). The woman, as a member of the Body of Christ, surprises Satan and his evil powers with a spiritual weapon of high impact in the heavenly regions. Having Jesus as Her Lord and Head and having learned submission to Jesus with her father, her husband or her spiritual leaders in God's family, she is restored to her spiritual position of dominion over principalities. Protected by a spiritual covering she recovers what she lost in the Garden of Eden when she was deceived by Satan. Again, remember that the woman is a figure of the Church, which walks in submission to Jesus, her Head, and receives His authority in the heavenly places (Eph.1: 21).

Satan understands this powerful truth and the serious consequences working against him. That is why he works hard to keep woman from positioning herself under spiritual authority. Clearly, he does not want to see women restored to their place of dominion. Sadly, many women are still trapped by him, as they keep fighting against the position established by God in Creation, which is filled with God's grace. Likewise, some parents and husbands, who do not understand their roles as spiritual authorities accountable to God, fall into this same deception when they try to exert oppressive dominion over women. These extreme positions must be revised through the correct understanding of the Word of God.

## Lessons in Nature

Nature created by God teaches many spiritual lessons to mankind. Paul points out natural signs that *teach* us about the spiritual positions of authority of men and women.

*Does not the very nature of things teach you that if a man has long hair, it is a disgrace to him, but that if a woman has long hair, it is her glory? For long hair is given to her as a covering* (1 Cor. 11: 14-15).

Paul was not giving doctrines about dress costumes or hair styles for men and women in the Church, but he was revealing something deeper about spiritual authority, which was hidden in the natural world. In our daily lives as we walk by men and women, we should be reminded by their natural look about the positions of spiritual authority established by God. This is called natural revelation (Rom. 1: 18-21).

*Every man who prays or prophesies with his head covered dishonors his head. And every woman who prays or prophesies with her head uncovered dishonors her head—it is just as though her head were shaved. If a woman does not cover her head, she should have her hair cut off; and if it is a disgrace for a woman to have her hair cut or shaved off, she should cover her head. A man ought not to cover his head, since he is the image and glory of God; but the woman is the glory of man* (1 Cor. 11:4-7).

The teaching of the apostle is clear: man must not cover his head; woman must cover hers. Paul says that men and women are allowed to prophesy and to pray. This is a summary of the ministerial activity: people speak to God though prayer, and to people through prophecy. Paul's point is: Christ must receive all the honor and glory through the ministry of men and women. He explains how.

## On Man's Position

Man was created with a natural sign on his head which shows his position in creation:

*Does not the very nature of things teach you that if a man has long hair, it is a disgrace to him?* (1 Cor.11: 14).

Paul says that "the very nature of things teaches" us that the use of long hair was disgraceful to man, in the same way that it was disgraceful for a woman to have her head shaved off (vs.6). The apostle talks about an impropriety based on nature itself, not on cultural patterns of the society, to argue for the covering of woman and for the uncovering of man.

The word he uses refers to a necessity founded upon an inner fitness of things. It is better rendered "proper." According to it, short hair for men and long hair for women is a divine suggestion in nature itself. Long hair does not fit the nature of man. It is not that man's hair cannot grow long. Paul is not saying that it is either good or bad, but that nature teaches that way.

The use of short hair, or sometimes even boldness, is an external sign on man's head of his spiritual position of authority, that the content of his prophecy or prayer comes straight from Christ, and that he is not being controlled by anyone, but Christ. It means there is nothing between man and God. Man is directly responsible to God for himself, and for his wife and children. What really matters is if he is submissive to Christ and positions himself as the spiritual authority and guardian of his family. This is the real meaning of the "uncovered head." A man honors Christ when he submits to Him and when he exercises spiritual authority over his children and wife. If he does it under the authority of Jesus and according to the model established by Him, he will be qualified and approved to minister in Church with authority, thus he will glorify Jesus. It will be clear to everyone that he receives his authority from the Lord, and that his authority has already been proved to work in the family he was given to govern. He will be accountable to God for the family God entrusted to him. Man is only authorized to minister under these conditions, no matter what gifts he has, because submission to Christ is essential to minister.

The spiritual authority of such a man is recognized by his wife. She does not see it as oppressive male domination. She receives it as a blessing which gives her total safety. His children also recognize his leadership and submit pleasantly to him. The results of his ministry are precious: if his authority is recognized at home, so will it be in Church.

Metaphorically speaking, a man covers his head or allows it to be covered when he neglects his spiritual leadership in the family or gives it to his wife. On such occasions, he is signaling in the spiritual world that Christ is not his head. If he ministers under such conditions, either at home or at Church, he is carrying out his ministry without the required authority from Christ. This is a spiritually dangerous position and he should not expose himself nor the Church he leads to it.

## On Woman's Position

Woman brings into her own nature a specific sign of her need for a spiritual covering, which is long hair:

*…but that if a woman has long hair, it is her glory? For long hair is given to her as a covering* (1 Cor. 11:15).

Who gave long hair to woman? Her Creator did! She was given long hair, not man. It was given to her because it fits her nature of woman. God Himself made that distinction. Metaphorically speaking, when a woman submits to her husband's spiritual authority and walks in accountability to him, she has her head covered and honors him as her head. She also honors Christ, who is honored when a man is free to exercise his spiritual leadership. When Eve was deceived by Satan and made an isolated decision, spiritually speaking she covered Adam's head, and uncovered hers.

When a woman covers her husband's head by being unaccountable, controlling, or rebellious, she dishonors the husband, Christ and herself. It is as if the head of Christ Himself was covered, denying His authority over the Church and His kingship already established at the cross.

The break up of the order of things is the principal reason why Satan is so interested in seeing disunity in a marriage. When it happens, Christ is dishonored. The rebellious wife dishonors her husband, and in turn, dishonors Christ and God, by obeying and pleasing Satan. That is at the heart of the instruction Paul gives to women in 1 Cor.11:5, 6:

> *And every woman who prays or prophesies with her head uncovered dishonors her head—it is just as though her head were shaved. If a woman does not cover her head, she should have her hair cut off; and if it is a disgrace for a woman to have her hair cut or shaved off, she should cover her head.*

## The Meaning of Covering

It is important to clarify the meaning of the word used by Paul and translated as "covered". The Greek word means "watched over,"[9] meaning "guarded and protected". It is not a passive religious word. It requires action from both husband and wife.

The husband's responsibility is to watch over his wife. It is a ministry full of dedication, and he has to do it with all his heart. He is supposed to keep spiritual vigil over his wife as a devotional exercise, to be attentive, to intercede, to keep guard and to take care of her, as he does his own body. It is a ministry of sacrifice in love. It is not an oppressive and controlling dominion to block her from serving God. His model is Jesus Christ, as Jesus Christ loved His Church:

*Husbands, love your wives, just as Christ loved the Church and gave Himself up for her to make her holy, cleansing her by the washing with water through the word, and to present her to himself as a radiant Church, without stain or wrinkle or any other blemish, but holy and blameless. In this same way, husbands ought to love their wives as their own bodies. He, who loves his wife, loves himself* (Eph. 5: 25- 28).

The head of a woman must watch over her as Christ watches over His Church. This attitude is real love put into practice. If a man does not watch over his wife, he will not be able to present her as his glory before Christ. She can only become his glory if she is well cared for. Anything less will bring dishonor to him. Christ will present His glorious Church before God because He takes care of her as His own Body (Eph. 5: 27).

The wife's responsibility is to accept and receive her husband's covering of protection, submit, and walk in accountability to him. Having this in mind, Paul requires a decision from Christian women: learn how to submit to your husbands because they are watching over you. By submitting, you will have your heads covered and the door of your houses closed to Satan.

Through obedience and submission the Corinthian women recovered their spiritual authority over the principalities of darkness dominating the city; they showed the evil spirits that they were free to serve the Lord Jesus Christ by ministering to that society in a saintly and godly way. Thus their heads would be covered.

You may be thinking…and about the single and unmarried women? To whom are they subject? What did the Law have to say about them? How do they learn submission?

## Single and Unmarried Women

The Church of the New Testament cared about the orphans and widows as if they had been adopted by the Church (Acts. 6:1-4; 1 Tim. 5: 3-6). When it was necessary, their spiritual covering was provided by the Church and its leadership. The Church, as God's family, had an important role in those cases.

In the loving community of a Church, orphaned, divorced and widowed women who did not have the opportunity to practice submission in their homes, or who failed the lesson for being rebellious or controlling at the time they had fathers or husbands, can have new opportunities to learn submission and practice it. As they submit to one another and to the Church's leadership, they are approved and authorized by God to consecrate their lives to ministry. In cases like these, the Church leadership is accountable to God for spiritual decisions made by orphaned, divorced and widowed women.

Women who have not learned submission, may get new opportunities to learn it in new relationships and as they submit to their spiritual leaders in the Church. This is a sowing and reaping process. The woman sows the seed of submission and accountability, and reaps authority to minister.

## The Theological Basis for Paul's Teachings

After giving the instructions for men and women, Paul presents the theological basis which is the order of creation:

*For man did not come from woman, but woman from man; neither was man created for woman, but woman for man* (1 Cor. 11: 8, 9).

## The Real Meaning of the Veil

Women who wanted to minister in Church would only be able to do so if their behavior was opposite of the women who controlled pagan temples. As we have already mentioned, pagan priestesses had their hair cut or shaved off. They were under the deception and dominion of Satan and his demons. The use of a veil or of long hair in Corinth was an important external demonstration of the new position believing women had in Christ.

However, there is a deeper spiritual meaning in this instruction. Even fallen angels had to recognize the new spiritual identity of those women printed in their submissive hearts as they lived out their lives at home and at Church. They watched the ministries of those women, once stolen in the Garden of Eden by the deceiver, now completely restored. All the powers of darkness, principalities and angels, and even Satan, had to acknowledge the new position and spiritual authority in the heavenly places of those women seated with Christ. And what's more, the powers of darkness had to submit to the women, because of the power and the authority given them by Jesus Himself.

This fact left Satan and his angels distressed and discontent, and we still see that today. Their entire spiritual environment was dramatically affected by the death and resurrection of Christ. They had to watch the victorious Christ crossing the heavenly places heading to God's throne and bringing along the risen Church, including the women He had liberated. God is the one who gives the final word in the battle for the authority over women. In order to show this, women should use the spiritual veil of submission to their spiritual authorities, as unto Jesus.

The veil is not a piece of silk or lace, but a powerful spiritual covering. It works as a spiritual law that is in full operation in the heavenly realms, which brings extraordinary results for women's lives. These are the powerful effects of the veil of submission.

The metaphor of the veil hides a spiritual secret, and it is a fundamental piece of women's spiritual attire which protects her as a single daughter, a wife, a widow, or an orphan, and that qualifies her to minister. The lesson of submission learned and practiced at home qualifies every Christian woman for ministry in any stage of her life. Her consecration is valid to God. Having learned submission, whatever her civil status, age, race, or skin color, she is prepared and authorized by God to minister in His Church. After all, her head is covered. The same veil is applied to the Church as the Bride of Christ. As the Church submits to Christ, it receives spiritual authority from Christ, her Head.

## The Use of a Veil of Earthly Fabric

If a woman wants to wear a physical veil made of fabric as a sign of her submission to her spiritual authority, she should not be prohibited. If another woman desires to use long hair, she should be allowed to.

In both cases, however, women should understand that the most important "veil" is the spiritual one, learning submission and practicing it in their daily lives. Otherwise, the observance of the veil or of the long hair will work only as an outward adornment or an act of religiosity. It will not add anything to her worship to God, to her ministry in Church or to her testimony before the principalities of darkness. The apostle is quite radical: *If a woman does not cover her head, she should have her hair cut or shaved off* (1 Cor. 11:6a). In other words, if she does not walk in submission, it would be better to have her hair cut or shaved off, than insist on wearing a physical veil.

Those who desire to wear a veil or long hair will not find any biblical prohibition. But they should not make it an issue of contention, for the apostle warns us not to do anything as an act of obligation or as a legalistic costume (1 Cor. 11:16).

In the same way, women who do not desire to wear a veil or long hair will not find any biblical commandment against it. This decision is only about personal hair style, it is not a spiritual decision. There is freedom to have long hair or not, to wear a veil or not. But there is no freedom to not wear the spiritual veil; no freedom from obedience and submission.

Summarizing: with or without the veil, with long or short hair, women are supposed to be submissive before the Lord in their homes and in all areas of life as an act of worship to God. When God watches their submissive hearts, He receives it as true worship and grants them the right and spiritual authority to minister to His family – His Church. He trusts them to speak in His name. They can then preach, prophesy, pray, and minister with every gift in every task or office to which they are called. They are authorized by God Himself.

Those who oppose the ministry of a woman should carefully rethink their position. When a woman has her head covered, and has learned submission she has God's authority to minister, and those opposing her will be accountable to God, who has called, gifted, empowered and anointed such women.

## Women in Church Government

At this point one may ask if God can call a woman to be in the government of a Church. Can a woman be a lead pastor? This is a very relevant question. It would require another book to answer it thoroughly.

Briefly, as we have seen so far, if a woman has learned submission and if she keeps walking in submission to her spiritual authority, she is qualified and authorized by God to serve Him in any type of ministry in the Church.

The passage of 1Timothy 3:1-2 immediately comes to mind when one thinks about the ministry of elders in the Church.

*Here is a trustworthy saying: If anyone sets his heart on being an overseer, he desires a noble task. Now the overseer must be above reproach, the husband of but one wife, temperate, self-controlled, respectable, hospitable, and able to teach.*

Interestingly enough, Paul starts the instruction to Timothy saying that "anyone" could eventually desire to become an overseer in the Church. Anyone seems to refer to either men or women. The problem comes when in the next sentence he mentions that the overseer should be "the husband of but one wife." It could be implied that the apostle is saying that an overseer should be a man, since he has to be the husband of one wife only. It would have to be implied also that an overseer should be married. If this conclusion were true, women and single men would be out of the question, and they would not qualify for the "anyone" the apostle uses at the beginning of the passage.

We have to be very careful not to imply things that are not been said in the text. In fact, Paul is not saying that an overseer must be a man. By the way, at the very beginning of the instruction he says that anyone could desire to serve in that noble task. So, how can we understand this apparent contradiction in the passage?

## The Polygamist Male World

We have to understand the cultural world where Paul was living and ministering. Let's remember that he was writing a letter to Timothy, the beloved disciple he had left in the city of Ephesus, to help the Christian Church get through a difficult phase victoriously.

Ephesus was a city of the pagan world. Polygamy was a widespread practice for men. Monogamy was quite a new concept in those times, especially in a gentile pagan city. Israel was slowly taught about it, and it took some time for God to take polygamy out of the Israelites heart and culture. In the pagan world monogamy was still a concept to be planted in people's lives. It would yet take years, perhaps centuries to accomplish it.

Christians were expected to set the standard and teach the world the commandments and the holiness of God. Therefore, an overseer, if man, should be the husband of one wife. That kind of instruction should not be given to women in a polygamist male world, for obvious reasons.

If we would accept that Paul meant that only men can be overseers based on the fact that in his instruction he only mentions men, how should we interpret the following passage about marriage?

*A woman is bound to her husband as long as he lives. But if her husband dies, she is free to marry anyone she wishes, but he must belong to the Lord. In my judgment, she is happier if she stays as she is—and I think that I too have the Spirit of God* (1 Cor. 7:39-40).

Paul does not mention "man" in this passage. Should we understand that he teaches that this instruction applies only to women? Of course not! Such an interpretation of Paul's teaching, would be speculative through The Hermeneutic of Silence, and it will not be able to hold its ground when compared to other biblical passages about marriage.

If in 1 Timothy 3 Paul was also implying that single men could not be overseers, he would be disqualifying himself to be one, since he did not have a wife (1 Cor. 9:5). And if that were true, not even Jesus would qualify to be an elder in the Church of Ephesus.

We must leave this delusion behind and clarify that the instruction from Paul to Timothy points to the following principles for the appointment of elders: 1) anyone may be an overseer –man, woman, single men; 2) if a man wants to become an overseer, he must be the husband of only one wife –he could not be a polygamist; 3) the same standard will be required from a married woman. Of course there was no need to include women in that instruction because polygamy was only practiced by men.

## Plural Leadership Model

Another important aspect related to the whole teaching of this book is that the New Testament teaches and exemplifies the government of a Church as ideally shared by a team of ministers. The Church of the first century practiced a plural leadership model. The government of Churches formed during the New Testament times was immediately entrusted to a body of elders. Those elders were responsible for the nurture and for the government of the local Church.[10]

When Timothy went back to Ephesus to set the Church in order, there were no Church buildings. We learn from history that buildings for Christian worship were not built until two hundred years later and were not commonplace until Constantine ended the persecutions of Christians. In those days Churches usually met in the homes of Christians. Thus, the thousands of Christians in and around Ephesus, did not meet in one central location, but in hundreds of small groups in homes. To be an elder in the Church at the time Paul was writing this letter did not mean the same as a senior pastor of our days. An elder who would oversee the Church would be a shepherd qualified by his or her personal life and walk with the Lord, holy and above reproach, and the ability to teach others.

This model is not normally practiced by present day churches for different reasons. It is clear, though, that plural leadership is the most accurate reflection of the biblical model of Church government. All Churches should purpose to move toward it, especially in the Cell Church movement. It may be acceptable for a Church to practice other models for a limited time, but only until all the circumstances are in place for the formation of a local presbytery capable of taking the governing function.

## Christ is the Head of the Church

The most important concept in the government of a Church is that Christ is the Head. There is only one Head in the Church, and that Head is neither a man nor a woman. It is Christ. Only a plural leadership can really guarantee that the full mind of Christ is shared with the Church through the diversity of ministries and gifts the elders receive from the Head.

In conclusion, men and women who are called, qualified, submissive and authorized by Jesus to be ministers can be part of such a model of Church government.

## Chapter Eight

# The Veil of the Wife
## 1 Corinthians 14: 33-35

*For God is not a God of disorder but of peace. As in all congregations of the saints, women should remain silent in the churches. They are not allowed to speak, but must be in submission, as the Law says. If they want to inquire about something, they should ask their own husbands at home; for it is disgraceful for a woman to speak in the church* (1 Cor. 14:33-35).

This is the most controversial text Paul wrote about women. Many wish he had never written it. For the integrity of this study and to be faithful to the meaning of the passage, we will examine it within the safe guardrails of biblical interpretation principles. According to these principles, a text must be understood within its context and any interpretative conclusion must always find biblical support in other Scriptural passages. Such procedures will guarantee that the interpretation is biblically sound.

## Is There a Contradiction in Paul's Teachings?

Before moving forward, we want to confess that the Word of God is true and never contradicts itself. Apparently, the above passage contradicts what Paul wrote before in chapter 11. Since we do not believe that Paul was confused, we have to study his instruction following the same path of thinking that he took to arrive at his conclusions. One thing is for sure: he was not prohibiting women to prophesy or to preach in church. It is clear in his previous instruction that women can pray and prophesy in church under certain conditions. Let's recall that instruction:

*And every woman who prays or prophesies with her head uncovered dishonors her head. ...Judge for yourselves: Is it proper for a woman to pray to God with her head uncovered?* (1 Cor. 11: 5-13).

We carefully examined this text previously and concluded that a woman can pray and prophesy in church, if she has already learned how to walk in submission and account-ability within the family. The integrity of her spiritual and ministerial life is guaranteed if she has proved to be teachable in learning submission to the order of authority established by God, which governs family life. If Paul did not prohibit women to pray and prophesy in chapter 11, but authorized it under some conditions, it is quite obvious that he would not contradict himself in chapter 14 and bring doubts and confusion to the church. There is only one being interested in confusion in the church, and that is Satan. Only Satan gains advantage from confusion and misunderstanding. Then what can Paul's instruction in chapter 14:33-35 mean? The only way to eliminate all the mistaken interpretations that surround this passage is by diving deeply into the spiritual and cultural context of the Corinthian church until we find the answer.

## The Church of Corinth

The church of Corinth was facing confusion and division. In almost his entire letter, Paul used strong words out of his apostolic authority to give the Holy Spirit's instructions to correct the situation. Until chapter 10, the letter has an exhortative character. Paul wants to correct the wrong ideas and practices which opened the church's door to deception. The main correction would be about how the order of authority works in God's kingdom.

The church did not understand that there is an order of authority that governs church life. They especially misunderstood how to operate in the spiritual gifts in the church service. They did what they wanted and when they wanted. Even the Lord's Supper instructions were misunderstood in the church. They did not discern the Body of Christ. The Lord's House was in disorder and this allowed deception and division to come inside; because every time there is disorder about authority, there is also division. As in a home, when the lines of authority are not clear, the family may split.

Some people were prophesying and teaching in the church services as if they had been commanded by the Holy Spirit. They were walking according to men and speaking as mere men (1 Cor. 3). Some had apostolic preferences and formed apostolic parties. In such a situation, it was hard to hear the Holy Spirit's directions to be sure about who was submitting to Him and truly speaking in His name. Division entered the Corinthian church through deception, which entered by a disregard for the order of authority.

## Disorder at Home, Disorder at Church

The Holy Spirit revealed to Paul that men and women were not walking according to the order of authority at home. That was the origin of the disorder of the church. Men were not exercising their positions of spiritual authority under the headship of Jesus Christ. Women were not positioning them-selves under the spiritual authority of their husbands. The disorder inside the marriage family was brought to God's family. The same disorder operating in their houses was transferred to the House of God. Thus, both men and women were not authorized to minister in church. Thus, decep-tion made its way easily into church life, bringing spiritual disorder along. The open door was rebellion against God's order of authority.

## Setting the Family Back in Order

Paul wrote chapter 11 to teach that there is an order of authority established by God that governs family life. This order is a spiritual law for life which has serious conse-quences for church life. This order must be respected for the good of the institution of marriage and for the good of the ministry of the church. It was mandatory that the Christian families of Corinth bring their houses back to that order. Otherwise, God's House would continue in disorder. That should be their priority: setting the House of God back in order by setting their own houses back in order. That was the clear meaning of the teaching. It was not a prohibitive instruction for ministering, but a positive plea to follow God's order for life.

## Setting God's House Back to Order

From chapter 12 on, Paul seeks to correct the disorderly state of the church by teaching how men and women should serve the church with their spiritual gifts. What he is teaching is that as in the natural family, there is also an order of authority to be respected in God's family. The Holy Spirit, who is the One who gives spiritual gifts as He wishes, is also the One who determines the order for everyone to serve and to speak in church for the edification of all. God's family is not a place for confusion, division and disorder. There is an order to be respected, and that is the order of the Holy Spirit.

## Christ is the Head and the Church is His Body

The figure of the body is a picture of the functions of men and women in the church. As in the marital relationship the man is the head and his wife is the body, so it is also in the spiritual union of the church with Christ. He is the Head and she is the Body. Although the Body of Christ is one whole unit, it is formed by individual men and women.

*The body is a unit, though it is made of many parts; and though all its parts are many, they form one body. So it is with Christ. For we were all baptized by one Spirit into one body—whether Jews or Greeks, slave or free—and we were all given the one Spirit to drink. Now the body is not made up of one part but of many* (1 Cor. 12:12-14).

Independent of race, nationality, skin color, or gender and social, civil, or political status, when men and women become new creatures in Christ, they are merged into one unit that submits to Jesus Christ. In the Body of Christ all are equal members. When all drink from the same Spirit, then all will be ministered to by Him, like when a person drinks water, all the parts of her body are visited by that water and receives its nourishment and refreshment. When all drink from the Holy Spirit, only the Head of the Body will be prominent and glorified in everything this Body does. That is the responsibility of the Holy Spirit in the church ministry: to make sure that everyone drinks from Him and that Jesus is glorified in everything. That is His order. Any other teaching or practice is to be considered as disorder in the church.

His order is not an obligatory silence during the church service, nor is it the way the furniture is arranged in the building. But it is the way the Holy Spirit administers the expressions of His gifts in the church service for the edification, consolation, and strengthening of every person who is in the meeting. This administration promotes the exaltation of the Person of Jesus Christ in the church (1 Cor. 14:26, 31).

The order of the Holy Spirit is that no one who comes to a church service should leave without drinking from Him through the ministry of men and women He gifted for that purpose. The Holy Spirit, who knows the hearts of all people who come to the service, will instruct His gifted servants to minister a word of wisdom, a word of knowledge, a word of doctrine, a healing, a prophecy, an interpretation of tongues, a psalm, and a revelation. This ministry happens at His command, through whom He commands, at the time He commands, and to whom He commands. If His order is obeyed, no one will leave the meeting without receiving ministry from Him. All will be edified and Christ will be glorified.

## There must be Unity in the Body

There must be unity among the members of the Body of Christ as there is among the members of a human body. Paul used the organic and harmonious figure of a human body to teach how Christians should experience unity. Unfortunately, the Corinthian Christians were not discerning this truth yet. On the contrary, there was a sharp contrast between the unity desired by God and the division operating in the Corinthian church. There was division in the Body in Corinth instead.

*You are still worldly. For since there is jealousy and quarreling among you, are you not worldly? Are you not acting like mere men? For when one says, "I follow Paul," and another, "I follow Apollos," are you not mere men? What, after all, is Apollos? And what is Paul? Only servants, through whom you came to believe— as the Lord has assigned to each his task. I planted the seed, Apollos watered it, but God made it grow. So neither he who plants nor he who waters is anything, but only God, who makes things grow. The man who plants and the man who waters have one purpose, and each will be rewarded according to his own labor. For we are God's fellow workers; you are God's field, God's building* (1 Cor. 3:3-9).

In this passage, Paul discerned that the division occurring in the church was due to the fleshly way the Corinthian Christians were walking. Paul said that they were walking according to men. That situation was distorting the image of Christ as the Head, for in a divided Body, how could one understand who speaks from Christ and who is under His authority? How can one discern the headship of Christ in such a Body?

Paul reveals that the origin of the parties in the church is their spiritual immaturity. They were worldly Christians who were dealing with church affairs in the flesh. Are not flesh and immaturity also the origin of the sexist[11] movements in the church of today?

## No Member has a Superior Position in the Body of Christ

Christians in Corinth were disputing which apostle should have the credit for the foundation of the church and which one should receive the most honorable title. Sounds familiar to some of our contemporary church's issues? Though Paul, Peter, and Apollos were on that man-made list, Paul would have nothing to do with the deceptive spirit reigning in the church. He would not be part of the dispute and would not be running for election to be proclaimed the most anointed one.

This situation seems to be common in many churches of today. Leaders are running for positions and titles such as: The First, The Anointed One, The Apostle, or The Church President, The Senior Pastor. No one strives to be: The Last, The Minor Apostle or The Servant of All. Sadly, many called to be servant ministers have become lobbyists instead. Any church walking in these ways is fleshly and immature; it is in disorder, lacks the discernment of the Body of Christ, and has to repent.

Paul explains that no member has a superior position in the church, neither him nor Peter or Apollos. They are only servants of God. The superior position in the church belongs only to God, for He is the One who brings growth to His own field.

*So neither he who plants nor he who waters is anything, but only God who made things grow* (1 Cor. 3:7).

The apostle exhorts with authority:

*Don't you know that you yourselves are God's temple and that God's Spirit lives in you? If anyone destroys God's temple, God will destroy him; for God's temple is sacred, and you are that temple* (1 Cor. 3: 16, 17).

God's temple must be built upon only one foundation, which is the Person of Jesus Christ (3: 11), not upon any other person, not even Paul. God's temple is sacred, for the Spirit of God dwells in it. The gifts operating in the members of the church are proofs of God's dwelling. No one should be exalted over others, because no one has a gift that has not been given by God. No one should desire to receive the glory due to Christ__ neither man nor woman. Only Christ should be exalted. He is the only One who is worthy to receive the honor and the glory in the church.

## The Unity of the Body of Christ and the Correct Expression of the Spiritual Gifts exalt Christ's Position as the Head

In the passage of 1 Corinthians 3, Paul called the church "God's field" and "God's temple." In 1 Corinthians 12, he introduces a new title: the Body of Christ. Through this metaphor, he shares a deeper revelation with the Corinthian Christians.

*There are different kinds of gifts, but the same Spirit. There are different kinds of service, but the same Lord. There are different kinds of working, but the same God works all of them in all men. Now to each one the manifestation of the Spirit is given for the common good. To one there is given through the Spirit the message of wisdom, to another the message of knowledge by means of the same Spirit, to another faith by the same Spirit, to another gifts of healing by that one Spirit, to another miraculous powers, to another prophecy, to another distinguishing between spirits, to another speaking in different kinds of tongues, and to still another the interpretation of tongues. All these are the work of one and the same Spirit, and he gives them to each one, just as he determines. The body is a unit, though it is made up of many parts; and though all its parts are many, they form one body. So it is with Christ. For we were all baptized by one Spirit into one body—whether Jews or Greeks, slave or free—and we were all given the one Spirit to drink. Now the body is not made up of one part but of many* (1 Cor. 12:4-14).

Paul makes some important points about unity: First, the church's unity is to be understood through the unity of the members of a human body (12:15-19). Second, unity is only experienced through the distribution of the Holy Spirit's spiritual gifts (12:1). Third, unity will be expressed in the church's life through the manifestation of the spiritual gifts under the coordination or order of the Holy Spirit (12:11a). Fourth, unity should be expressed in love (chapter 13).

A church that prohibits the expression of the gifts of the Spirit and concentrates on one person's ministry does not exalt Christ as the Head of the Body. The correct expression of the gifts and the coordination of them under the order of the Holy Spirit lift Jesus as the highest name in the Church. There is no mention of the gender of the members of the

Body in the distribution of the gifts. The criterion is "as the Holy Spirit determines."

## When a Church becomes a Body

The church only becomes a body when, under the authority of the Holy Spirit, it functions as a body and the members know their place in it and exert their functions exactly and perfectly as in a human body. Without Him, the church cannot function as a body. There are many local churches, but not many operate as a body. The Church of Corinth was an example of a dysfunctional body.

In order for Christ to be recognized as the Head, men and women have to discern their places and functions in the Body of Christ, apart from distractions such as race, skin color, social position, profession, age, gender, and civil or political status. That is because it is a spiritual Body.

Only when all members of the Body can express themselves in a healthy way and in unity, the Head of Jesus Christ is lifted up high. Paul wants Jesus to be exalted above all. That is Jesus' wish in his prayer to God in John 17:

*My prayer is not for them alone. I pray also for those who will believe in me through their message, that all of them may be one, Father, just as you are in me and I am in you. May they also be in us so that the world may believe that you have sent me* (Jn. 17:20, 21).

## Love is the Ideal Temperature for the Exaltation of Jesus

Paul desires that every one in the Corinthian church experiences the spiritual gifts for the edification of the entire church and for the exaltation of the name of Jesus. This is the highest form of worship and exaltation of Christ. He speaks of it at length in chapter 12.

In chapter 13, he introduces the teaching of the absolute necessity of love for the practice of the spiritual gifts in the church. He explains that love is the only permanent donation of the Holy Spirit. All other gifts have a temporary life span. They are vital for the life of the church now, but they will cease when they are not necessary any more; that is, when we all will be known as Christ knows us now (13:12b). When that time comes, only the permanent gifts will remain. Love maintains the ideal temperature for the preservation of the position of Christ as the Head of the Body.

## The Gifts of the Present Season

Paul calls the church's attention to the correct expression of spiritual gifts. The current gifts of the Holy Spirit have a temporary nature and a partial function in the church today. Their temporary nature is shown in these verses:

*Love never ceases. But where there are prophecies, they will cease; where there are tongues, they will be stilled; where there is knowledge, it will pass away. For we know in part and we prophesy in part, but when perfection comes, the imperfect disappears (1 Cor. 13:8-10).*

Their partial functionality is shown in these verses:

*Now we see but a poor reflection as in a mirror; then we will see face to face. Now I know in part; then I shall know fully, even as I am fully known (1 Cor. 13:12).*

All spiritual gifts are absolutely essential for the present ministry of the Holy Spirit in leading and ordering the church as Jesus Christ desires. But they have only a partial ability to reveal everything as it really is. That is why Paul refers to their function as "imperfect" (1 Cor.13:10b). This present period of time is called by Paul "*now*" in contrast with another period called "*then.*"

### The Gifts of the Future Season

There will be a future time referred to by Paul as "then" when Christians shall see face to face and know fully. There is only one biblical possibility for the meaning of this time of "then."

Paul explains it to us:

*When I was a child, I reasoned like a child. When I became a man, I put childish ways behind me* (1 Cor. 13:11).

Paul likes using figures of speech to express the most profound biblical truths. Here he uses the figure of a child who will eventually become a man. Maturity brings mature ways of life, and the child puts the childish ways behind him.

### The Infant Church of *now*

A child with her childish mentality, feelings and ways is a figure of the present church, which is temporarily in the world. In this period, the knowledge and the revelation of the church are partial. The church does not know all yet, but it does know the things that have already been revealed and that belong to us and to our children (Deut. 29:29). In this period, the church walks according to the Word of God and the ministry of the Holy Spirit. This is the childhood or the *now* time.

## The Mature Church of *then*

But there will be a time of maturity when the spiritual gifts will be left behind. That will happen when we see Jesus Christ face to face and the revelation about Him will be made complete and perfect. This is the ultimate purpose for the church in its union with Jesus, as Paul reveals to the Ephesians:

> *...until we all reach unity in the faith and in the knowledge of the Son of God and become mature, attaining to the whole measure of the fullness of Christ. Then we will no longer be infants...* (Eph. 4:13, 14a).

The mature man is a figure of the church of the future season, which will have full knowledge of the Person of Jesus Christ. The Apostle John also spoke of this future time by the revelation of the Holy Spirit, in a very simple way:

> *Dear friends, now we are children of God, and what we will be has not yet been made known. But we know that when He appears, we shall be like Him, for we shall see Him as He is* (1 Jn. 3:2).

Paul reveals which gifts will remain for the future season of the church:

> *And now these three remain: faith, hope and love. But the greatest of these is love* (1 Cor. 13: 13).

He exalts the gift of love among the other three. Why is love the most excellent of all? Here is the answer.

## Love is the Ideal Temperature for the Expression of the Diversity of Gifts

In the future season, our position and ministry will be determined by love, not by gifts. Paul warns us even now to use gifts associated with love, otherwise we will gain nothing. Faith and hope will be concrete, and love will remain. Its value never ends. It is eternal (1 Cor. 13:8).

The Corinthians should continue operating in the gifts of the Holy Spirit during the present time. But they should learn that the only gift that will never end is love. Because of that, they should grow in the practice of the gift of love, as they exercise their other spiritual gifts. Love maintains the ideal spiritual temperature for the practice of the diversity of gifts that preserves the visible position of Christ as the Head of the church. Only love can cause the members of the Body to consider others superior to them and to be able to submit to the order of authority at work in the church. As well as the only way to submit or to exert spiritual authority in the family and in the church is through love.

## Following Paul's Steps

We reach chapter 14 with Paul's view about the church as a spiritual body which is growing towards maturity. One may be wondering at this point if the theme of this book has been left behind. After all, what does all of this have to do with the submission and authority in the church? We will understand it soon. In this chapter we have to walk step by step through the same path Paul took to instruct the Church of Corinth. As I mentioned before, this is the only way to understand the passage that we want to study in this book's chapter (1 Cor. 14:33-35).

In the two previous chapters (12 and 13), Paul exposed his theology of spiritual gifts and in chapter 14, he offered examples for applying the theology into effective practice in church ministry. We have to understand that Paul is no longer discussing either the possibility or the prohibition of women's ministry. That is not even in his mind at this point. He already covered that subject in chapter 11. He is then giving instructions about the order of the Holy Spirit for the operation of spiritual gifts in the church service.

The principle teaching is that all operations of spiritual gifts have two purposes: to exalt the Person of Jesus Christ and to edify the entire church.

*So it is with you. Since you are eager to have spiritual gifts, try to excel in gifts that build up the church* (1 Cor. 14.12).

Knowing this, we will proceed now to understand the meaning of Paul's instruction in chapter 14:34, 35.

## The Understanding of the Voices spoken in Church is Crucial to the Unity of the Body

Paul teaches that all sounds, voices, and languages have their own meaning and importance. A sound, a voice or a language must be understood by someone in order to have significance and importance. Understanding the sound or the voice is absolutely essential:

*Again, if the trumpet does not sound a clear call, who will get ready for battle? So it is with you. Unless you speak intelligible words with your tongue, how will anyone know what you are saying? You will just be speaking into the air* (1 Cor. 14:8, 9).

The apostle explains that as there is meaning in all voices and sounds in the world, there is also meaning in praying

and in singing in other languages (1 Cor. 14:10). These practices have meaning and edify the spirit of the Christians (1
Cor. 14:14). But there is no meaning for those who do not
understand the language (1 Cor. 14:16). If there is no understanding, there is no edification (1 Cor. 14:7). And it is imperative that everyone be edified in the church's meetings.

*What then shall we say, brothers? When you come
together, everyone has a hymn, or a word of instruction, a revelation, a tongue or an interpretation. All
of these must be done for the strengthening of the
church* (1 Cor. 14:26).

**Submission to the Holy Spirit guarantees that only
Christ's Voice is spoken in Church**

Only the voice of Christ needs to be clearly heard in the
church. It is the only way to avoid confusion. His directions
to the church must be absolutely clear and understood. The
Holy Spirit's ministry will make sure that happens. Remember
that in the Church of Corinth everyone could talk and share
their opinions and by doing that they were causing division.
The voice of Christ was not clear. In the next section Paul
elaborates the point he is making.

*For you can all prophesy in turn so that everyone
may be instructed and encouraged. The spirits of
prophets are subject to the control of prophets. For
God is not a God of disorder but of peace* (1 Cor.
14:31- 33a).

All *can* prophesy. But all *must* be taught and encouraged.
The most important result in the church gathering is that all
must be edified through teaching or consolation. That is
why all can prophesy. There must be freedom in the church

service for the Holy Spirit, who knows all hearts and needs (and even if there are unbelievers present in the meeting), to use anyone He wants to minister. This way, under the order (or command) of the Holy Spirit no one will be forgotten in the distribution of the spiritual gifts.

The Holy Spirit will use all, men and women, to distribute the manifestations and expressions of His ministry to each one, as He wishes. The distributions of the Holy Spirit have pre-determined targets: those who need to be edified in the congregation.

*All these are the work of one and the same Spirit, and he gives them to each one, just as he determines* (1 Cor. 12:11).

## The Holy Spirit Determines the Order of Speaking in Church

For the distribution of expressions and manifestations of His ministry to the church, what matters is not race, age, gender, skin color, or social position of the instruments He chooses to use. What does matter is if they are submissive to the Holy Spirit and willing to hear His voice and to follow His order. Those who do not meet these qualifications should not speak in church, no matter which gift they have or what their gender are. The gifts are not meant to be personalized; they belong to the Holy Spirit.

The sequence presented by Paul is "in turn" or "one after another" (1 Cor. 14:31). He gives practical common examples of the church life:

*What then shall we say, brothers? When you come together, everyone has a hymn, or a word of instruction, a revelation, a tongue or an interpretation. All of these must be done for the strengthening of the church. If anyone speaks in a tongue, two—or at the most three—should speak, one at a time, and someone must interpret. If there is no interpreter, the speaker should keep quiet in the church and speak to himself and God. Two or three prophets should speak, and the others should weigh carefully what is said. And if a revelation comes to someone who is sitting down, the first speaker should stop. For you can all prophesy in turn so that everyone may be instructed and encouraged. The spirits of prophets are subject to the control of prophets. For God is not a God of disorder but of peace. As in all the congregations of the saints, women should remain silent in the churches. They are not allowed to speak, but must be in submission, as the Law (1 Cor. 14:26-33).*

Therefore no one should speak in church except if the Holy Spirit commands to do so, because the distribution of consolations, teachings, revelations and healings, for instance, is determined and ordered (sequentially) by Him (as He wishes). In each example given in the above passage, Paul asks for moderation in speaking.

### The Expression of the Gift of Tongues must have Interpretation

No more than two or three should speak in a spiritual language, one at a time and with interpretation. If there is no interpreter, the speaker should *keep quiet* in the church, and speak to himself and God (1 Cor. 14:27, 28). That is because the Holy Spirit wants everyone to be edified, and tongues without interpretation do not edify all.

## The Expression of the Gift of Prophecy must follow the Sequence of the Holy Spirit

*Two or three prophets should speak, and the others should weigh carefully what is said. And if a revelation comes to someone who is sitting down, the first speaker should stop* (1 Cor. 14:29-30).

These instructions demonstrate that Paul wants all to understand that the Holy Spirit is the One who determines the order of the church service. If He gives someone a word of prophecy, the one who is speaking should stop or *be quiet*. It is clear that if this happens, it will be because the first person is speaking either too much or out of order. The Holy Spirit would never command someone, who is speaking His word in His order, to be quiet.

## The Order of the Holy Spirit rules in the Church Service

The instruction to speak one at a time is given in order to avoid the confusion which was part of the church services in Corinth. Some were speaking as they wanted, disregarding others present in the meeting, even of unbeliever guests (1 Cor. 14: 23). Some evidently would even try to control the meeting without giving opportunity to others. Paul encourages all Christians to be quiet instead of speaking in the church. If someone speaks, *it must be only under the order (command) of the Holy Spirit and according to the order (sequence) determined by Him.*

This is the central point of the passage. It is astonishing that some churches disregard it when they meet. When men and women meet in the love of Christ for worship services; when the edification of each other is priority in the meetings; when there is spiritual discernment and judgment of what is spoken in the church (to discern if it is the Holy Spirit who speaks); then there will be unity. All will be edified, the unbelievers will be saved, the sick will be healed and the name of Jesus Christ will be glorified. It will be clear then, that the expressions and manifestations of the gifts come from Jesus Christ, the Head, to His Body, through the order of the Holy Spirit.

The Holy Spirit receives all the instructions from the Head of the church and transmits and administers them to the Body by means of the gifts in operation in the church.

## Women Will Speak According to the Order Established by the Holy Spirit

The instruction of the Holy Spirit for women in this passage is of an administrative order and not of a restrictive order. First, they must have learned how to operate under the order of authority at home; then, they will be able to operate under the order of the Holy Spirit at church.

This is the meaning of the following instruction, which is the one that interests us most for the purpose of this book. It refers to women in the church service. Paul keeps using firm and strong words, which is a characteristic of this letter. It is appropriate to quote the passage here again:

*Women should remain silent in the churches. They are not allowed to speak, but must be in submission, as the Law says. If they want to inquire about something, they should ask their own husbands at home; for it is disgraceful for a woman to speak in the church* (1 Cor. 14:34, 35).

The issue of submission as determined by the Law seems to be inserted in the instruction without any apparent reason. But this is only an impression. The inclusion makes sense and it is properly placed in the text. Submission of a woman means submitting or placing herself voluntarily under the same mission given by God to the couple, which is administered by her husband. The submission of wives is of vital importance for the proper order of the family, because it is the order of authority established by God that governs family life.

In the above passage, the order of authority for a family is brought into the context of the church. This means that God's order of authority is also vital for the good order of the church service. As I have previously mentioned, this instruction does not define the woman's function, but establishes the order of the Holy Spirit for her to speak in church.

This shows the integrity and coherence of Paul's view of women. They can only speak in church if they have learned submission at home. Because the order of creation establishes the order of authority in the family, a woman can only pray or prophesy in church (bringing now this text in harmony with 1 Cor. 11), if she has her head covered; that is, if she is authorized to do so.

The veil of submission is an essential piece of the spiritual wardrobe of a Christian woman. It is a piece of protection for her ministry in church. The same protection that it brings to her personal and family life is extended to her church. It is a matter of responsibility before God and the church for a woman to wear it. It is not optional for her to have a teachable spirit for learning submission, if she wants to minister in church. It is not only about her marriage life. It is also about her ministry in church. Her behavior at home directly affects her life in church. The same principle is valid for single and widowed women. If they do not have parents or husbands, they are supposed to have learned submission at home anyway.

Therefore, a non-submissive woman shows her own irresponsibility and rebellion if she insists on ministering in church. She should rather be quiet. If she is rebellious, she is vulnerable to deception and can put the whole church at risk of deception. As she uncovered her head at home, she can uncover the church, which will dishonor her and Christ. That is when it is disgraceful for her to speak in church. She has only two options: be quiet or learn how to dress herself with the veil of submission. When she learns it and is approved, she is authorized to minister. The spiritual veil that protects her family will also protect her church.

## Order at Home, Order at Church

All, men and women, can speak in the church service. They must speak in turn, each one at a time, quickened by the Holy Spirit. They will be judged by the others. But women (single, married, widows, etc.) can only speak if they have already learned to walk in submission at home. Otherwise, it will be disgraceful for them to speak in church (1 Cor. 14:35b). It will be as if they had their heads shaved.

The Holy Spirit will use women who already submit to the order of authority. In this way, they close the door to deception entering in the church, at least through them. What determines if they can speak or not in church is if they are dressed with the veil of submission.

In summary: the Holy Spirit will use a woman to pray or prophesy, but only in the Spirit's order. Otherwise, she should remain quiet in church. It is a matter of order. She must first learn submission at home to then speak in church. Rebellious women should remain absolutely quiet in church. They are not allowed to speak. First, they have to repent and then go back home to learn how to submit to their spiritual authority. The order of the Holy Spirit must be obeyed.

This principle is so important that it also applies to men. If men are not submissive to Jesus Christ; if they are not spiritually governing their families; if they are not walking in submission to one another in the church; and if they are not following the order of the Spirit, they must remain quiet in church (1 Tim. 3:5). It is not the gift that authorizes someone to speak in the church. It is not someone's gender either. But it is the Holy Spirit. And His authorization is only given to women and men who walk in submission.

# Chapter Nine

# The Veil of the Minister
## 1Timothy 2:11-14

W hen Paul wrote this first letter, the church of Ephesus was in danger. False teachers had invaded the beloved church where Paul had taught for three years (Acts 19:8, 10; 20:31). They brought deception, confusion, heresy, and much damage to the flock. The apostle had warned the church elders in the Millet meeting that after his departure from Ephesus, wolves would come in the church.

This was his alert:

*Be on guard for yourselves and for all the flock, among which the Holy Spirit has made you overseers, to shepherd the church of God which He purchased with His own blood. I know that after my departure savage wolves will come in among you, not sparing the flock; and from among your own selves men will arise, speaking perverse things, to draw away the disciples after them. Therefore be on the alert* (Acts 20:28-31a).

That warning became a reality soon and some immediate action needed to be taken. Paul asked Timothy to remain in Ephesus and set the House of God in order, for *"the household of God, which is the church of the living God is the pillar and support of the truth"* (1 Tim. 3:15b). Timothy would be Paul's representative to correct error and to instruct the church. The apostle sent him instructions on how to proceed in that situation. This is what the first letter to Timothy is all about.

It is crucial to understand the purpose of the letter to understand the text we are studying now.

## Spiritual Warfare in Ephesus

Paul's alert was clear—wolves would attack the flock. He meant that Satan would come against the church. Those wolves arose from among the flock and it is likely they were elders of the church. Timothy's mission was as important as it was difficult, and he would have to be bold, courageous and firm in the faith, because it would involve warfare against maligning forces.

## Fighting False Teachers

They wanted to be teachers of the Law, even though they did not understand either what they were saying or the matters about which they made confident assertions (1 Tim. 1:7). Those false teachers were conceited (1:7; 6:4), contentious, and engaged in controversial questions and disputes about words (1:4; 6:4). They were straying from the truth (1:6a), falling away from the faith (4:1a), and paying attention to deceitful spirits and doctrines of demons (4:1b). They were hypocritical liars, seared in their own consciences with a branding iron (4:2). They took advantage of their religious positions to get financial gain (6:5b, 10). Following such practices and their favorite demons, they fell into deception and a snare and wandered away from faith (6:9-10).

Paul sent radical instructions to Timothy to implement the appointment and ordination of ministers. The Ephesians should uphold the qualifications required for someone to minister and teach God's family (3:1-13 and 5:17-25). The teachers of the Word should be carefully selected. They should receive double wage and all their needs should be provided for (5:17-18), for they had the responsibility to keep the teaching of the Word sound and healthy. The church could not afford to have more false leaders coming into ministry and damaging the flock of God.

## Fighting False Teachings

Timothy was fighting against false doctrines (1:3; 6:3); myths, endless genealogies and mere speculation (1:4); fruitless discussion, worldly and empty chatter, and opposing arguments of false knowledge (1:6; 6:20); worldly profane fables (4:7). The teachings forbade some practices and actions created and blessed by God (4:3) and contradicted and opposed the Wisdom of God (6:20).

Beyond all of those, Timothy was also facing envy, strife, abusive language, evil suspicions, and constant friction between men of depraved minds deprived of the truth (6:4, 5).

## Timothy's Position for Fighting

The situation was not pleasant for a young pastor to face. He would have to take a firm position of spiritual authority, be constant in faith and be irreproachable. He would have to be vigilant about himself and the doctrine (4:16) and learn how to be content with what he owned (6:6-8). He was supposed to be a good model for all (4:12-15) and submit to God's Word.

*This command I entrust to you, Timothy, my son, ...fight the good fight, keeping faith and a good conscience, which some have rejected and suffered shipwreck in regard to their faith* (1 Tim. 1:18a,19).

## Timothy's Weapon for Fighting

Timothy would have to focus on reading and teaching God's Word in order to correct deception and false doctrines (4:13). Only the truth of God's Word could break through the evil works in progress within the church (John 8:32). Deception would be the main adversary of Pastor Timothy in this spiritual battle. Paul wanted to make sure that Timothy had the weapon in proper condition to defeat Satan:

*In pointing out these things to the brethren, you will be a good servant of Jesus Christ, constantly nourished on the words of the faith and of the sound doctrine which you have been following. But have nothing to do with worldly fables fit only for old women* (1 Tim. 4:6-7).

*Prescribe and teach these things....Until I come, give attention to the public reading of Scripture, to exhortation and teaching. Do not neglect the spiritual gift within you, which was bestowed upon you through prophetic utterance with the laying on of hands by the presbytery. Take pains with these things; be absorbed in them, so that your progress may be evident to all. Pay close attention to yourself and to your teaching; persevere in these things; for as you do this you will insure salvation both for yourself and for those who hear you* (1 Tim. 4:11a, 13-16).

There were two main doors of the church to be guarded from attacks: the teachings of the Word and the teachers of the Word, through whom the teaching was ministered to the church. Paul's letter focuses on these two main subjects.

## Refocusing the Church's Mission to the City

The above brief description of the church's situation will help us understand the instructions given in chapter 2, which is the text we want to examine for the purpose of this book. Make no mistake about it; Satan's ultimate intention in Ephesus was to interrupt the mission of the church to the city, by creating a teaching disorder. He knows that when a church is in disorder, it cannot reach out to the city, as a family in disorder cannot minister to the church, either.

The Church of Ephesus was not reaching out to the city, because it was involved in too many indoor debates and disputes about controversial arguments and words (1:4). That was Satan's master plan and his demon-teachers were the guest speakers in those debates. That situation was very disappointing because by that point in History the entire city of Ephesus should have already been conquered for Christ, and the church should have been advancing with the Gospel to other regions. However the vision had been lost among the ideas of deception and division. How could a church sidetracked by confusion be able to set people free from deception?

Timothy was the Holy Spirit's chosen one to reverse that situation. His priority was clear: he should restore the church's identity, doctrine, and position in the kingdom of God, in order to have her engaged again in the evangelization of the city. The church should once again preach the

Gospel with boldness and spiritual authority, as Paul had done when he was there (Acts 19:8; 20:25).

## Mission's Weapon of Combat

In chapter 2, Paul's focus is the mission of the church to reach out to the people of Ephesus, which would include intercession and evangelization outside the doors of the church. The apostle discloses to the church how spiritual combat takes place in the heavenly realms, how the church will position itself, and which weapons it will use in order to defeat Satan and conquer the city for Jesus Christ.

### Invading the City by Intercession in the High Places

Paul commands the church to intercede to be victorious in its mission to the city.

*I urge, then, first of all, that requests, prayers, inter-cession and thanksgiving be made for everyone— for kings and all those in authority, that we may live peaceful and quiet lives in all godliness and holi-ness. This is good, and pleases God our Savior, who wants all men to be saved and to come to knowledge of the truth. For there is one God and one mediator between God and men, the man Christ Jesus, who gave himself as a ransom for all men—the testimony given in its proper time* (1 Tim. 2:1-6).

The exhortation focuses the task of evangelization. The church should know that God's desire is that all men be saved and come to the knowledge of the truth. When men and women trust in the Gospel, they are saved, their lives are changed and they transform their families and cities (Ps.2:1-4; 33:12). Because spiritual combat for the city's redemption starts in the heavenly regions, the church should start out by invading heaven with strategic and objective intercession to set people free from Satan's deception. The church would conquer the city by defeating Satan in the heavenly places in the first place.

Paul was determined to break down the structure Satan had developed in the church, which was delaying it from conquering the city. Timothy had to undermine Satan's structure at its base. This foundation was formed of false ministers who were learning from demons and teaching the church. Following the Holy Spirit's directions, Paul establishes a powerful strategy for Timothy to implement through the church.

*Therefore I want the men in every place to pray, lifting up holy hands, without wrath and dissension* (1 Tim. 2:8).

In other words, Paul is saying this: "Satan tried to keep you from accomplishing God's mission for the city's redemption by snaring you through deception and division. Now, purify your lives and hands, stop debating over demons' teachings, overcome wrath against each other by forgiveness. Go out with your hands and relationships purified; start praying and interceding for the souls of people every where. Conquer your city for Christ."

The first place for the church to visit is God's Sanctuary in heaven through prayer and intercession in the name of Jesus Christ (Heb. 4:14-16; 10:19-25). When the church is positioned and seated with Christ in the heavenly realms it is *"far above all rule and authority, power and dominion, and every title that can be given, not only in the present age but also in the one to come"* (Eph. 1:21; 2:6). From that place of dominion and authority in Christ, the church fights against principalities and powers of darkness and sets people free.

In his own letter to the Church of Ephesus, Paul sent instructions about how the combat against those powers of the enemy should be fought:

*Put on the full armor of God so that you can take your stand against the devil's schemes. For our struggle is not against flesh and blood, but against the rulers, against the authorities, against the powers of this dark world and against the spiritual forces of evil in the heavenly realms. Therefore put on the full armor of God, so that when the day of evil comes, you may be able to stand your ground, and after you have done everything, to stand* (Eph. 6:11-13).

To these things they should associate holiness (lifting up holy hands), forgiveness (being set free from anger), and unity of faith (stop disputing), which are absolutely fundamental for achieving victory in the battle for a city. A church that offers the forgiveness of Jesus and reconciliation with God outdoors must live that way indoors. Its testimony will be irreproachable and its spiritual authority unquestionable by the people it ministers to and especially by the opposing spiritual forces of darkness.

The church of Ephesus should awake from its long sleepiness, passivity, and lethargy provoked by unending discussions. The church, once assaulted and deceived by Satan, should surprise him with an attack to destroy his points of dominion in the city and set free the people he kept chained.

The church should use the powerful, effective, and untraceable weapon of intercession. The Ephesians Christians should learn that the gates of Hades cannot prevail against the church, as Jesus had taught His disciples (Mt. 16:18). Paul wants all Christians taking their positions and fighting through intercession in the streets of Ephesus and bringing into the church the best of the enemy's spoil, the kings, all who are in authority, and all the men they can (1 Tim. 2:1, 2), for this is the Will of God, and it is good and pleases Him (1 Tim. 2:3, 4).

*This is good, and pleases God our Savior, who wants all men to be saved and to come to knowledge of the truth.*

## Men's Combat Position

Men are instructed to invade heaven with intercession after having purified themselves, forgiven others and having ceased all disputing over doctrines (1 Tim. 2:8). Under such conditions, they would be free and authorized by God to engage in combat and to be victorious.

## Women's Combat Position

Women were authorized to pray in church (1 Cor. 11:2. 5). Could they also pray in public in the streets and be engaged in combat for the city's redemption? The Apostle Paul answers it:

*The same way, I also want women to dress modestly, with decency and propriety, not with braided hair or gold or pearls or expensive clothes, but with good deeds, appropriate for women who profess to worship God (1 Tim. 2:9-10).*

When Paul says "the same way" he is talking about praying outdoors and reaching out to the city with the Gospel of Jesus Christ, and we should understand that he is authorizing women to engage in that kind of prayer. The conditions required for men are the same for women: holiness, forgiveness, and unity of faith.

Besides that, women should pay close attention to discretion and modesty in the way they dress and present themselves. They should go out in the streets of the city, not to show off themselves and their expensive clothes and hair style, but to show the love of God through the practice of good deeds and godly actions in love. Jesus should be seen in the streets through them, because they would be going out to pray and to exert spiritual authority over the principalities and powers at work in the city.

Instead of wearing an apparatus of attire, women should bring the external sign that they were covered by the veil of submission and were authorized to minister with spiritual authority. That sign would be recognized and acknowledged by the demons who would have to submit to the ministry of those women and set people free from their bondages (1 Cor. 11:10)! The veil of submission, which is their covering, becomes their veil for ministry. That is the meaning of the following instruction of Paul:

> *A woman should learn in quietness and full submission. I do not permit a woman to teach or to have authority over a man; she must be silent* (1 Tim. 2:11).

We have to follow Paul's thinking and theology on women as we interpret these verses. He did not create a teaching for the Church of Ephesus different from the teaching for the Church of Corinth. Women can pray in Ephesus as they can pray in Corinth and in any other place in the world, if they have learned how the order of authority operates in the kingdom of God. This order does not allow women to use the spiritual authority that belongs to their husbands. Make no mistake about it; Paul is referring to the authority of a husband over his wife. He is not talking about any man. If a woman had not yet learned how to submit to this order, she must be silent. This is the context of this instruction. She is not allowed to go out and face the spiritual battle for the city if she is not covered and authorized for it. She may become prey instead of a conqueror. This instruction was given in order to protect the spiritual lives of women. Again, it is an administrative instruction and not a restrictive one.

If women learn and submit to the order of authority at home, acknowledging the spiritual authority of their husbands, they are well dressed for ministry, covered with the veil of submission. They will not be deceived, but will have victory against the enemy. In that case, they can go and fight the spiritual battle in the streets.

## The Theological Basis for the Instruction

*For Adam was formed first, then Eve. And Adam was not the one deceived; it was the woman who was deceived and became a sinner* (1 Tim. 2:12-14).

The order of creation is recalled by Paul as the basis for his teaching. We should also recollect it at this point to proceed to our conclusion. Remember that the order of creation established the order of authority. This order is a spiritual law in operation in the whole universe, and it is recognized even by demons at work in the heavenly realms of the city. Only those who respect and submit to this order are authorized to minister in the church and in the city.

This was particularly important to minister in a city where deception was in operation, even inside the church. Women should pay double attention to that order. That is why Paul says: "And Adam was not the one deceived; it was the woman who was deceived and became a sinner" (2:14). This is a difficult statement for women to read, but it is a true declaration of the Scriptures, to which all have to submit. Paul spells out their limitation — a potential or an inclination to invert the roles of the order of authority established by God and be seduced by deception. This is the woman's nature after the Fall. Of course, women redeemed by the blood of Jesus Christ do not need to follow their fleshly nature. They can overcome it by the power of the Holy Spirit and be a blessing and a messenger of truth to the Body of Christ and to the peoples of the earth. But rebellious and controlling Christian women are susceptible to fall into the same trap that Eve did.

It is important to notice that Paul is not saying that deception comes in the church through women only. As a matter of fact, in the Church of Ephesus, it seems that deception and heresy had been introduced by men. In other letters of the New Testament, there are warnings and prophecies about men who would attack the Church of Christ with false teachings and prophecies (2 Tim. 2:15-18; Tit. 1:10-16; Jude 1:4, 10-16). But the apostle wants to make sure that all the doors of the church are safely locked against deception, because Satan will keep trying to enter through deception again, as he did in the Garden of Eden when he seduced Eve to open the gate to him.

## Men and Women can ministry to the city

In conclusion, men and women can pray and preach in the streets, transform their society, and minister to the nations, after having learned how to live in holiness, forgiveness, unity of faith, and in submission to the order of authority established by God. Dressed with propriety and covered by the veil of a minister, women are authorized by God to go to all nations and exert spiritual authority against principalities and powers and present people from every nation redeemed before God. There are no barriers or impediments to their ministry. Their ministry field is wide open, from home to church, from church to the city and to the nations.

## Chapter Ten

# The Veil of the Mother
### 1Timothy 2: 15

In the same first letter to Pastor Timothy, Paul reveals another secret behind the veil of submission. It is a truth that comes from God's throne as a powerful weapon to resist Satan's attack against a woman's family, especially her offspring. Here is this secret:

> *But women will be saved through childbearing—if they continue in faith, love and holiness with propriety* (I Tim. 2:15).

### The Problem Created by a Woman's Rebellion

We already know that Satan's intention in the Garden of Eden was not only to lead the man to disobedience and to introduce sin into the world, but he especially targeted the woman and led her to rebellion with the purpose of dishonoring Adam and thus, God. The astute plan of Satan took advantage of Eve's desire to gain wisdom to become like God (Gen. 3: 5, 6). Eve's lack of spiritual discernment to understand God's plan was then exposed. She was deceived about God's command given through Adam and about its meaning and purpose. She was snared by Satan. The Apostle Paul clearly stated that Adam was not the one deceived; it was the woman who was deceived and became a sinner (1 Tim. 2:14).

However, God charged Adam with the responsibility for the entrance of sin in the world, because he was his wife's head and also sinned (Rom. 5:12). God put them together to accomplish their mission on earth but Eve forsook her position. God was forced to discipline Eve but He did it as part of His divine grace and purpose. Since then, her husband has spiritual authority over her. The serious consequence was that God's plan for filling the earth with a people He could fellowship with was dramatically affected.

### The Solution Brought by a Woman's Submission

The sin of Adam and Eve was very serious and God dealt with its consequences by sending His Son, born of a woman to save humanity. Through the motherhood of Mary, Jesus — the salvation of all mankind — was brought into the world (Gen. 3:15). Through a woman by the way!

When God sentenced the serpent, He told him that from that point on there would be enmity between him and his offspring and the woman and her offspring. God was explaining that Satan would persecute the woman and her descendents. They would not have good relationship any more as they had in the garden. But the woman would be blessed and a blessing through the childbearing. The prophetic promise was a reference to Jesus' birth from a woman and to the justice that would come from Jesus to restore the spiritual condition of men and women.

Eve brought sin to the world. Mary, another woman, brought life to the world by giving birth to the Savior of the sins of the world (Matt. 1:21). God restores the woman's condition by means of Mary's motherhood. Mary was submissive to God's plan and Jesus was born from a divine conception (Lk. 1:35-38). Mary's submission contrasted with Eve's rebellion. Mary proved to humanity that it was possible for a woman to do God's will and to be a vessel of God on earth.

## Overcoming Satan through Childbearing

*But women will be saved through childbearing — if they continue in faith, love and holiness with propriety* (1 Tim. 2:15).

This is the spiritual secret Paul reveals in 1Timothy 2:15: women can defeat Satan's persecution against their offspring and raise holy children who will have fellowship with God. Paul uses the pronoun *she* to refer to a woman. The Greek text reads: *"if she remains..."*[12] that is, the woman, Eve, and every woman who is her descendent, will be saved or restored if they live in faith, love and holiness. In other words, Paul says: "Women, do not go back to Eve's position. You have already been restored. Learn how to walk in faith and according to your position and you will raise children to God."

The apostle is not referring only to the physical circumstances of motherhood, such as, the nine months of pregnancy, the pains of childbirth, the nursing and the baby's cries during the night. He is referring to the spiritual responsibility of a mother's mission to take care of the children God entrusted to her. She is supposed to take care of them as God Himself would do. She is supposed to raise God's descendants as obedient children to Him and His Word who will reflect His image as sons of God. In order to accomplish such a mission, a mother needs to live a life as a child of God who is submissive to Him and His Word. As we have seen in the previous chapters, a mother learns that kind of submission in her walk with her husband, who is the spiritual authority over her life.

If a woman positions herself under God and the spiritual authority who watches over her life in submission, she will be given spiritual authority to raise her children. They will walk in submission and not in rebellion. Her authority over them will not be only because of the order of creation factor, but also and mainly because of the spiritual authority released by God to her life because of her submission. Her authority does not need to make use of physical strength or threats to force their obedience. Her authority is totally spiritual and overflows from her life and walk with God. It is a fruit of her spiritual sowing: she planted the seed of submission and she reaps authority in her children's lives. They will listen to her instructions because of her spiritual authority delegated by God to teach them in His ways. She will raise them in the discipline of the Lord. Rebellion will not enter her house to seduce her children. Satan will not have the power to harm them and lead them to rebellion, because she is a woman of submission. She missed the point in the Garden of Eden, but she will not miss it now, in her own family garden.

A woman who has not yet learned the ways of submission should not think about getting married before learning it. She should not even consider having children before she learns it. Otherwise, she will expose her offspring to rebellion and to Satan's deceptions. Raising children is a very serious spiritual mission given to women, and they have to understand that it can only be well accomplished by spiritual men and women.

The angel of rebellion will come against the Christian families to try to seduce their children. When they see the veil of submission over their mothers and the spiritual authority that radiates from that, they have to flee and leave those children alone. Rebellion will not find a foothold to go through. The gate of this garden is well protected.

## A Woman of God's Trust

When a woman learns how the spiritual law of authority works and submits her life to it in obedience to God, she is able to raise children obedient to God. As she raises the children God entrusted her with in her family, she gets God's approval and trust to take care of His children in His family, the church.

Jesus, the Head of the Church, would not trust His spiritual authority conquered on the cross to rebellious women who do not understand the price He paid for it. If a woman wants to minister with and under the spiritual authority of Jesus, she needs to learn how to live and minister according to the spiritual law of authority. Jesus will only trust His authority to this type of woman.

The *rationale* is "if a woman has not yet learned how to walk in submission to her spiritual authority, how will she be able to walk in submission to Jesus? If she can not love her husband she can see, how will she love God she cannot see?" (1 Jn. 4:19, 20). Submission is the strongest and the most convincing expression of a wife's love for her husband, as well as of the church's love for Christ (Eph. 5:22-24).

Jesus trusts in a woman whose heart is inclined to walk in submission and whose children are obedient to their parents. As she is approved in the caring of her own children, in her first ministry field, God entrusts her to care for His children in His own family, which is the church. The veil of submission she wears covers her and her children now. Her mission is beautiful, unique and nontransferable. She is dressed for ministry and her clothing is magnificent. And Satan will have to admit it.

## For Men Only

God also requires particular qualifications from men before they are authorized to exercise their ministries in church:

*Here is a trustworthy saying: If anyone sets his heart on being an overseer, he desires a noble task. Now the overseer must be above reproach, the husband of but one wife, temperate, self-controlled, respectable, hospitable, able to teach, not given to drunkenness, not violent but gentle, not quarrelsome, not a lover of money. He must manage his own family well and see that his children obey him with proper respect. (If anyone does not know how to manage his own family, how can he take care of God's church?)* (1 Tim. 3:1-5).

As we have previously discussed, this text is to be applied to men and women. Paul focuses on the caring of the precious Church of God. A man is qualified to minister in the church when he has proved to be able to govern his own household with spiritual authority. The meaning of the rhetorical question in verse 5 is quite clear. It refers to a man who has not yet learned how to raise children who walk according to the authority established by God. He needs to prove that he is able to exercise his spiritual authority to raise God's descendants before taking care of God's church. A father is under the same spiritual law of authority that a woman is. He needs to learn how to walk in submission to Jesus, his head (1 Cor. 11:3) and to the spiritual authorities over his life; he needs to walk in submission to others in the church family; he needs to walk with his wife as a spiritual and accountable husband in order to be trusted with spiritual authority to minister to Christ's spiritual family.

The apostle is as radical to men as he is to women. If they do not know how to walk in submission to God, and to apply their spiritual authority according to the model of Jesus in their first family, their first ministry field, they will not be authorized to lead the church, which is God's family.

Much attention has been paid to the issue of the ministry of women in church, and almost none has been paid to the ministry of men. Generally speaking, the church has been partial to men in the discussion and conclusions on this subject. Such partiality is harmful and unbiblical. The biblical truth is that if a man does not have Jesus as his head and does not govern his family with the spiritual authority according to the model of Jesus, he is not qualified to take care of the Church of God — no matter how many gifts, degrees, titles, and experiences he might have. This is not a matter of gender! It is a matter of order ... spiritual order!

In conclusion, to take care of the church is a serious spiritual task. Men and women who are called for such a privileged ministry have to do it according to the conditions determined by God, because the church is His spiritual house.

## Chapter Eleven

# The Veil that Covers the Body
## Eph. 5: 22-23

I n his letter to the Ephesians, Paul presents a revelation about the church, which was kept hidden from the prophets of the Old Testament. The church, formed of newborn Jews and Gentiles, is pictured as a victorious church seated in the heavenly places with Jesus and invested of His power and authority. The church has a unique heavenly mission to accomplish with Jesus. The effectiveness and strength of the church resides in its union with Christ. Without Him, she can do nothing. But united, they will complete the mission to make known the manifold wisdom of God to the rulers and authorities in the heavenly realms (Eph. 3:10).

### The Union of a Couple is a Symbol of the Unity of Christ and His Church

In this revelation, the unity of Christ with the church is presented as a great mystery. In order to explain it, for the first time in his letters, Paul speaks of it through the figure of marriage. In his previous letter to the Corinthian church, Paul had lightly covered the teaching he gives to the Ephesians.

*I am jealous for you with a godly jealousy. I promised
you to one Husband, to Christ, so that I may present
you as a pure virgin to Him. But I am afraid that just
as Eve was deceived by the serpent's cunning, your
minds may somehow be led astray from your sincere
and pure devotion to Christ* (2 Cor. 11:2, 3).

Paul's purpose was to present the church of Corinth as a
pure virgin to Jesus, her only Husband. To the Ephesians, the
apostle goes further in this revelation and explains the mystery
of the intimate union of Christ and His church through the
figure of the intimate union between a man and his wife in
marriage. The biblical passage pictures it beautifully:

*Wives, submit to your husbands as to the Lord. For
the husband is the head of the wife as Christ is the
head of the church, his body, of which he is the Savior*
(Eph. 5:22-23).

The apostle's desire is that couples understand that their
union should mirror the union between Christ and His church.
The couple transmits to the whole church an image of how
Christ and His church should walk together. Their marriage
has an educational task to teach that truth to the whole
church. When a couple makes the unity between Christ and
His church an example to follow for their marriage, it will
become a valuable living teaching tool to the entire church.

Paul is talking about a marriage that is ideally designed
by God. Husbands should follow the example of Jesus as
the head; wives should follow the example of the church,
as the body. The marriage of Christian couples should be
examples for the church and for the world in restoring the
dignity, honor, and holiness of marriage. Sadly, this is not
always true. Men have forsaken their commitments before
God and despised and switched "bodies" many times and

women have also despised and switched "heads," bringing shame to the church and to the name of Jesus.

One of the reasons the church should preserve the honor and dignity of marriage is that it is a symbol of the unity between Christ and His church. This means that the husband should be a living example of Jesus, and the wife, a living example of the church. Of course, only a marriage between a man and a woman will do it. There is not even a remote chance to conceive of a marriage between two men or between two women achieving God's purpose for marriage. The biblical and holy unity of Jesus and His church must be expressed through the marriage of one man and one woman.

Paul affirms that it is possible for men and women to experience a glorious marriage. There is a truth about the mysterious union between Christ (the Head) and His church (the Body) that only Christian couples can understand through the unity of their marriage.

The text guarantees that if the Holy Spirit's instructions are obeyed by the husband and the wife, the unity of the couple will be preserved and they will live out God's perfect design for marriage.

We will examine these instructions separately for husbands and wives. Let us start with God's design for wives.

## For Wives Only

*Wives, submit to your husbands as to the Lord. For the husband is the head of the wife as the Christ is the head of the church, his Body, of which He is the Savior. Now as the church submits to Christ, so also wives should submit to their husbands in everything* (Eph. 5: 22-24).

There are important instructions for wives and for the whole church in these revealing verses. First, wives are instructed to **submit[13]to their husbands as to the Lord.** The Holy Spirit teaches that a wife is submissive to her husband in the first place, but ultimately, she is submissive to Jesus. Paul says "as to the Lord" because the head over her husband is the Lord, and thus, is her Lord too. In other words Paul is saying *"Wives, respect your husbands and submit to them, for as you do it, you are doing it to your Lord Jesus Christ."* She is learning how to walk in submission to Jesus as she learns how to walk in submission to her husband in daily life. Her submission is a pleasant sacrifice she offers to her Lord Jesus Christ. If she is a rebellious wife, she is also rebellious toward Jesus.

Paul repeats this same instruction to the church of Colossus:

*Wives, submit to your husbands, as is fitting in the Lord* (Col. 3:18).

Even though the meaning of the instruction is quite clear, it is important to emphasize here that a wife is expected to walk in submission (in the meaning of the verse) to her own head, who is her husband, not to every man in the church. In the same way, a man should not expect or require submission (in the meaning of the verse) from any woman who is not his wife.

A wrong teaching has been disseminated in God's Church by some people who believe that women should be submissive to all men in the church, only based on the gender factor. For the same reason, they conclude that women are not allowed to teach men in the church, leaving a very limited teaching ministry to women, which include women of every age, children, and boys until twelve years old, or any other age determined by the culture as man's age of maturity. Or some would say that God will allow women to teach in some missionary situations where there is no man ready to teach. (I have heard this from many people, and I have never found the Scriptural basis for such a concession.) This distorted teaching comes from incorrect conclusions drawn from the texts of Ephesians 5:21-22 and 1 Timothy 2:12, and must be rejected by the Church of God and corrected by the pure teaching of God's Word.

We should restate at this point that submission to the church's authorities, to the nation's authorities, and to one another in the church, is an indisputable biblical commandment of God's Word, but is not the subject of these two texts in question.

The second instruction for wives is that they should submit to their husbands *as the church submits to Christ.* The church's submission is the model for the wives' submission. This means that the wives should define submission to their husbands through the understanding of the way (or manner) the church should submit to Jesus. All who claim to understand Paul's teachings will agree that the real Church of Christ loves Him and delights in walking in submission to Him and in being led only by Him. That is because He is the One who loves her in a special way. Only Jesus gave His body for her and shed His innocent blood on the cross to save and purify her. The church trusts in His love for her, which is why she will walk in submission to Him. This is an unquestionable truth: the church's purpose is to understand Christ's will and direction and follow Him in complete submission, until the mission assigned to her is accomplished on earth. The church knows that she can only complete that mission in full cooperation with her Lord and Savior, who is her Head.

It is the same way a wife should feel about her husband. She should delight in being led by him and in submitting her life to him. This is quality submission. It is qualified by the same determination and trust that the church submits to

Christ Jesus. It is not an imposed, oppressive, or unwilling resolution. On the contrary, it is a determined and delightful choice to walk together with her husband and to accomplish the mission they received from God for life, as the church is Christ's partner for His mission on earth (1 Cor. 3:9; 2 Cor. 5:18-20; 6:1).

## The Biblical Submission Factor for Wives

The submission of a wife to her husband should be understood as a support for the accomplishment of the couples' mission in the edification of their Christian home, in raising Christian children, in serving the church as a unit, and in ministering the Gospel in love to the community where they live. This supportive role will be done in love, trust and accountability, under the headship of Jesus Christ as the Lord of the couple.

A better way to understand what God desires in a wife's submission is to know what he means and expects from His church. God's Word explains it to us:

> *After all, no one ever hated his own body, but he feeds and cares for it, just as Christ does the church—for we are members of his body. "For this reason a man will leave his father and mother and be united to his wife, and the two will become one flesh." This is a profound mystery—but I am talking about Christ and the church. However, each one of you also must love his wife as he loves himself, and the wife must respect her husband* (Eph. 5:29-33).

Jesus loves His church. He gave His life to save her and through His resurrection He took her to be seated with Him in His throne in the heavenly realms. He gave to her His own power and authority for the accomplishment of His mission on earth. He protects and takes care of her as His own body. He expects that His church will make a commitment to trust and follow His leadership (or headship) and to walk with Him for the completion of His mission on earth.

Wives are expected to make a similar commitment to their husbands. Of course, husbands are supposed to love and take care of their wives as Jesus does to His church. In fact, man and woman are expected to be submissive to the biblical model of marriage.

As we have seen, a wife is submissive to her husband in the first place, but she is ultimately submissive to Jesus. The submission of a wife is a pleasing sacrifice she offers to her Lord Jesus Christ.

## Implications for Women's Ministry

As the submissive church receives ministries and gifts from her Head Jesus Christ and can exercise them under His authority, a woman, who is a figure of the church, is also free to exercise her ministry and gifts in the church. At home, the relationship between a wife and her husband is of spiritual submission and accountability. In the church, ministry is determined by the calling that Jesus, the head of the church has given to both of them, and by the gifts the Holy Spirit distributes to them as He wishes. That is why in a church a woman can teach or preach to her own husband and vice-versa. The church is a spiritual Body and the criteria for ministry are spiritual and not gender related.

It is also relevant to notice that the Lord uses the figure of a "bride" for the church. The church as the Bride of Christ can only be understood in a spiritual way, especially by men. How can a man be a bride? In order to answer this question, a man has to understand that the church is a spiritual organism where there are no Jews or Greeks, no slave or free, neither male nor female. The Bride of Christ is a female figure of speech used to express that all of those who are included in Christ after having trusted in Him are now one spiritual being. This Bride is being prepared and sanctified to be actually part of Christ in a concrete way in the future events revealed by the Scriptures.

## The Most Profound Meaning of the Marital Union

There is a profound mystery in a marriage union as there is in the union between Christ and His church. A couple, who decides to live in obedience to the model for marriage that God prescribes, will experience not only the most profound meaning of marriage, but they will also deeply understand the union of Jesus and His Church. The right kind of spiritual leadership of a husband and the right kind of submission of a wife position the couple to understand this profound revelation of God. Because they are living out the most profound meaning of marriage as God designed it, they are able to spiritually comprehend the revelation about the union between Christ and His Church. As the apostle Paul said,

> *After all, no one ever hated his own body, but he feeds and cares for it, just as Christ does the church— for we are members of his body. "For this reason a man will leave his father and mother and be united to his wife, and the two will become one flesh." This is a profound mystery—but I am talking about Christ and the church. However, each one of you also must love his wife as he loves himself, and the wife must respect her husband* (Eph. 5:28-33).

## For Husbands Only

The head of a woman should exercise his spiritual authority following the example of Jesus Christ. In the same

way that Jesus treats His Church, a husband is expected to
treat his wife. The characteristics and qualities of Jesus, as
the Head of the church, are the ones a husband should try
to develop in his own life in order to qualify for the biblical
role of husband.

*Husbands, love your wives, just as Christ loved the
church and gave himself up for her to make her holy,
cleansing her by the washing with water through
the word, and to present her to himself as a radiant
church, without stain or wrinkle or any other blemish,
but holy and blameless. In this same way, husbands
ought to love their wives as their own bodies. He who
loves his wife loves himself. After all, no one ever
hated his own body, but he feeds and cares for it, just
as Christ does the church— for we are members of
his body* (Eph. 5: 25-30).

Husbands are commanded to love their wives with
the same nature of love that Jesus loves His church. It is a
profound, unconditional, sacrificial, merciful, gracious and
permanent love that bears everything until He can see His
own glory reflected in His church.

A husband, according to Jesus' model, will share his
life with his wife and will have as his life's purpose to love
her, save her from deceptions, protect her, take care of her,
and above all to present her as a radiant woman before His
Lord. A wife is part of her husband. They form one flesh. A
wife cannot resist this kind of love, and will spontaneously
respond in submission to this kind of husband. His irresist-
ible love will facilitate the appropriate dynamics necessary
to build up the kind of marriage God designed since the
beginning.

## For Christ's Bride Only

Since the church is formed of men and women, all are supposed to submit to Christ. This means that all who belong to the Body of Christ must learn the lesson of submission. Everyone, men and women, are learning submission to Jesus in the church as they submit to one another in love for the building up of the whole Body of Christ (Eph. 5:21). The exercise of the ministries of men and women in the church are released under the spiritual authority of their church leadership. Their ability to submit to Jesus is developed as they learn how to submit to their spiritual leaders. The author of the letter to the Hebrews teaches us on this:

*Obey your leaders and submit to their authority. They keep watch over you as men who must give an account. Obey them so that their work will be a joy, not a burden, for that would be of no advantage to you* (Heb. 13:17).

## For Church Leaders Only

The Word of God also teaches that church leaders will be accountable to God for the way they keep watch over their sheep. They should shepherd like Jesus Christ, the Supreme Pastor and Bishop of all souls (1 Pet. 2:25). The apostle Peter instructs leaders to shepherd God's flock as role models.

*To the elders among you, I appeal as a fellow elder, a witness of Christ's sufferings and one who also will share in the glory to be revealed: Be shepherds of God's flock that is under your care, serving as overseers—not because you must, but because you are willing, as God wants you to be; not greedy for money, but eager to serve; not lording it over those entrusted to you, but being examples to the flock* (1 Pet. 5:1-3).

Those who shepherd God's flock the way He commands will receive a reward when Jesus, the Chief Shepherd, appears: *And when the Chief Shepherd appears, you will receive the crown of glory that will never fade away* (1 Pet. 5:4).

## Chapter Twelve

# The Veil Made in Heaven
### 1 Peter 3:1-6

W e have arrived at the last text of our study. We will wrap up the biblical teaching about the relationship between wives and husbands and its implications for ministry.

*Wives, in the same way be submissive to your husbands so that, if any of them do not believe the word, they may be won over without words by the behavior of their wives, when they see the purity and reverence of your lives. Your beauty should not come from outward adornment, such as braided hair and the wearing of gold jewelry and fine clothes. Instead, it should be that of your inner self, the unfading beauty of a gentle and quiet spirit, which is of great worth in God's sight. For this is the way the holy women of the past who put their hope in God used to make themselves beautiful. They were submissive to their own husbands, like Sarah, who obeyed Abraham and called him her master. You are her daughters if you do what is right and do not give way to fear* (1 Peter 3:1-6).

This instruction of Peter becomes easier to understand, after comprehending the Pauline vision about the subject we are examining. A wife's proper submission and account-ability, demonstrated by a gentle and quiet spirit becomes a weapon to combat the powers of darkness which are keeping her husband away from obedience to the Word of God. Peter is referring here to two different types of men, the Christians who still resisted to God's Word in some aspects, and to the unbelievers, who had not yet believed in Christ and been born again.

## A Woman's Powerful Weapon

Peter is revealing one of the most powerful spiritual weapons a woman can use. Peter is addressing those women whose husbands may be Christians but are not yet positioned as heads of their families according to the model of Jesus, and those whose husbands are not yet born again. He wants to prevent wives from being disrespectful, controlling and rebellious toward their husbands. Some of those women could even desire to leave their families and justify them-selves by reasoning like this: "God is calling me to church ministry, so I have to leave my husband in order to conse-crate myself to it. After all, he does not understand my calling because he is not as spiritual as he should be to be my head. My only head is Jesus." This may sound spiritual, but is, in fact, a very subtle and self serving rebellious declaration. And we have already concluded that rebellion disqualifies a person for ministry. For "rebellion is as the sin of divination, and insubordination is as the iniquity of idolatry (1 Samuel 15:23).

Peter's passionate teaching says that a woman may win a great victory in the spiritual realms which will powerfully affect her home on earth. Her victory will depend on the spiritual position she decides to take. Without speaking a word, she is able to win her non-Christian husband or her disobedient Christian husband to Jesus.

Many women try to control their husbands by talking too much, by giving everyday sermons, or by persuading them through seductive weapons. In fact, attitudes like these are fleshly and may provoke a contrary effect, which is not what they really want to get. The "side effect" is serious contention between the couple, because of what I will call here, the dynamic of enmity. This dynamic is a system that was turned on in the Garden of Eden after the Fall, and it has been in operation since then, troubling men's and women's ecology of relationship.

## The Dynamic of Enmity

Sin is responsible for the introduction of enmity to the Garden of Eden: between God and man, man and the soil, and woman's seed and the serpent, who is Satan. Sin also brought enmity between man and woman. We can see this dynamic in many relationships. This is its rationale: *because in Eden the man listened to his woman beyond what he should, letting sin and death enter the world, now, when a woman speaks trying to control her husband, he has the tendency to not listen to her. Her attitude pulls a trigger inside of him and his reaction sets off contention.*

To certain measure, this reaction works as a defense system installed inside a man's spirit after the Fall, to avoid the pattern of behavior and the consequences which occurred in Eden. The alarm of this system sounds loudly as a husband fears loosing control over a situation or over the home.

When a wife persists against her husband in issues, and tries to be in control, her husband's internal defense alarm sounds off with contention. The result is predictable: he does not listen to her and locks himself in a contrary position, in order to not give up control. Then fear blinds reason. It is as if a kind of "Adam memory of Eden" came back in for just a few seconds and took over the situation. As soon as Eve comes into the scenario, Adam decides to play his part. The man's fear of loosing control often surpasses even his loving feelings for his wife. Ironically, he succeeds in not losing control to her, but he loses control to fear. The ecological disaster of relationships occurs again, now in the Garden of Marriage.

Many couples who truly love their partners are victims of this disaster which many times end up in divorce. They mistakenly conclude that love does not exist any more. The truth is that the "Adam terror" became operational and choked love to the point that it was hidden.

## Reversing the Dynamic of Enmity

The couple has to work together in order to reverse the effects that the dynamic of enmity has brought to their marriage.

The wife has to cast out the Adam "ghost" of fear which is terrifying her husband. This "ghost" has power to destroy the marriage. She is the one who has to provide her husband with the assurance that she is not fighting with him over control of the home and that she does not want to be the leader. She has to convince him that this fear has no reasonable basis. To do so, she needs to go back to her position as a submissive wife who sets her husband in the position as head of the home. At her fingertips is the button to eject the Adam terror out of the marriage. Submission in love is this powerful button. Her submission is the worthiest and strongest expression of her love, because it is what costs her the most.

The husband has to face the truth that fear gained control of his life. He must get rid of it and go back to experiencing real love for his wife, for "perfect love casts out fear" (1 John 4:18). The spiritual husband needs to clearly understand how this dynamic may work against him and his marriage. He must be alert and avoid letting the "Adam memory" and the "ghost of fear" take control of his decisions. He is head of the couple to lead the marriage by Christ's directions, by faith and not by fear. The spiritual man does not make decisions by his feelings. He listens to his God-given suitable helper, analyses her opinions and input, and then takes positions under the Holy Spirit's directions. He is the leader, but this does not mean that he is the one who has to decide everything for the family. He is not supposed to enforce his opinion all the time in every little detail. He is in a place to try to listen to God's Will, and that Will sometimes may come from God directly to him. However at other times, it will come through his wife, his suitable helper, who is heir of the same grace of life and of the same God-given mission.

## The Spiritual Leadership Factor

It is very important to stop at this point to understand what spiritual leadership means. Jesus was the first to talk about it. According to His teaching, leadership in the kingdom of God contrasts to the concept of leadership in the world, in the kingdom of men.

*Jesus called them together and said, "You know that the rulers of the Gentiles lord it over them, and their high officials exercise authority over them. Not so with you. Instead, whoever wants to become great among you must be your servant, and whoever wants*

*to be first must be your slave— just as the Son of Man
did not come to be served, but to serve, and to give
his life as a ransom for many* (Mat. 20: 25-28)

Kingdom leadership is different. I am so glad our Lord
Jesus Christ made it clear and also set the example for us to
follow. This model is good for everything inside His kingdom,
which means for the church, for the family, for Mission
Agencies, Christian Schools, Seminaries, Companies, etc.
This is the model Jesus Christ set up for Himself to be the
Head of the church, who is His Bride. Every man is supposed
to follow Christ's example to lead his family. He is not to
"lord over his wife," but to "serve her." What a spectacular
concept of leadership and government.

In a practical way, a husband's leadership task could be
described as a facilitator of the couple in order to understand
Christ's mind for the family. As such a facilitator he leads
the family with the spiritual authority that comes from Jesus,
because he is following His commandments and directions.
It is from Jesus Christ that his leadership comes. It is not from
himself per se. God gives man the natural gift of government
and Christ bestows on man the spiritual authority to lead the
family.

## Let Eve Die

The apostle Peter is aware of this dynamic as he teaches
wives to be silent and to pray instead of using words. In other
words, Peter is saying: "Wife, be wise! Do not try to convince
your husband that you have the right opinion or decision.
Pray to Jesus instead. And Jesus, who is the Head of every
man, will speak directly to him. He will listen to Jesus. Do
not interfere in the relationship of authority between Jesus
and man. Let the Eve nature inside of you die!"

## The Reward of Submission

It is relevant to state here that the Word of God does not talk about blind submission which does not discern the Will of God. God is the ultimate authority over all, including the will of the husband. There may be situations when a woman will face conflicts between the Word of God and the word of man. In such situations she will have to listen closely to God's Word and obey Him instead of man (Acts 4:19, 20).

Through the exercise of submission to her husband, a wife can reach a level of authority and dominion in the heavenly realms, which releases God's blessings for her family. This is the reward of her position of submission with faith and fear of the Lord. Far from being a passive and suffering type of attitude, it is an active submission, which is full of faith and trust in the Christ's authority that is over her husband__ for "Christ is the head of every man" (1 Cor. 11:3), even the non-Christian man. Her submission comes out of her spiritual wisdom and willingness to obey Jesus. She can see Jesus above her husband. She rests in this trust; and resting in God is not passivity at all. It is a rest that waits in Him with patience until God sends her the deliverance. Such a woman is ultimately submissive to Jesus as her Lord as she obeys His commandment to be submissive to her husband, even if he still does not obey the Word of God. She waits in prayer with a gentle and tranquil spirit, which is precious in the sight of God (1 Pet. 3:4b).

## More Effective than Prayer

God highly prizes this attitude of submission and gentleness of a spiritual woman. It seems to be even more effective than prayer. Apparently, while nobody is seeing it and nothing seems to be happening, God is rejoicing in her position and working secretly in her favor. He is preparing her a surprise. The reward of faith will be given to those who please the Lord with faith: "And without faith it is impossible to please God, because anyone who comes to him must believe that he exists and that he rewards those who earnestly seek him" (Heb. 11:6).

## Heavenly Dressed

This is what it means to be covered by God: He puts on her the veil made in heaven. This veil protects her while her husband is not yet prepared and able to cover her. Jesus himself covers her. It does not matter if she is divorced, orphaned, widowed, happily married, or not. Her God does not forsake her. He dresses her. He has zeal for her. She has a head, Jesus Christ Himself. He will not allow the enemy to deceive her or to lead her astray. He will honor His word to her. She has only to trust in Him and wait for Him.

The process of learning submission in cases like these may be painful and accompanied by tears. But if a woman remains on the tracks of intercession and submission, God will answer her prayer and give her the victory. Perseverance is her best friend for this walk.

Peter pictures this quiet and submissive attitude as a piece of clothing more precious than jewelry or sophisticated and expensive dresses. God highly values a woman dressed up like this. Dressed as God pleases, she will get a concrete blessing from Him: her husband's conversion or her husband's submission to God's Word. The heavenly veil protects her and her husband. It covers both of them.

When a wife understands and practices this teaching without trying to overthrown her husband's authority, she gives control of her marriage to Christ. By doing this, she spiritually protects her husband and preserves his head, free and open to Jesus' voice. She does not cover her husband's head, and does not prevent him from hearing Jesus.

## Not Eve's Daughter, but Sarah's

Peter says that this veil reveals the secret of a woman's beauty. This secret is not altered by fashion, age, popular philosophies, cultures, church costumes or by the last soap opera. It is a secret for all times, because it comes from the Word of God. And the Word of God lasts forever. This secret transforms a woman and makes her even more beautiful. The saintly wise women of the past discovered this secret, put it into practice and won their victories. Other foolish women lost even what they had already conquered for their lives by having not valued this secret of life.

There are many good biblical examples of the past, but Peter mentions Abraham's wife, Sarah. He reports that Sarah was submissive to Abraham and called him "lord". She did so because she understood that the government of the family was his. She walked safely with him and felt comfortable in following him, for she knew that the head of her husband was over him. Abraham did not even know where he was going (Heb. 11:8), but Sarah knew that God knew, and that was enough for her. Herein lies the key to a woman's trust and rest. Her husband may not know where they are heading, but she trusts that God, who controls everything, will lead him. She takes an attitude of total dependency on God. This position pleases God highly. Such a woman wins great capacity and boldness in her intercession before God.

Peter sees Sarah as the pioneer of a new generation of women. In fact, he calls her the mother of a new kind of daughters: the ones who do what is right and do not give way to fear. Abraham is called the father of those who have faith. Sarah is presented as the mother of women who are submissive to their husbands and who have faith in God.

Peter instructs wives to follow Sarah's example to become her daughters. This means that a qualitative transformation will happen in their spiritual lives. Wives who walk in submission by faith are transformed and are able to experience a new dimension in their spiritual journeys.

This is a spiritual decision that a woman must make. It is a decision to die in Christ in order to submit to the new life of submission to Him. As the church has to die in Christ and submit to Him as her Head, so a woman must go through the same process in order to be able to practice the real submission as a wife. The woman who learns how to walk this road will experience remarkable spiritual progress.

God will be pleased and will share deep intimacy with her. She will have prayers answered in a powerful way. Her husband will also be pleased as he sees the purity and reverence of her life full of God's fear, and he will be spiritually transformed. Her children will obey her and follow her example of submission. She will raise children and prepare them to serve the Lord.

Such a woman is rescued from rebellion to submission and from frustration to victorious life. She is no more a daughter of Eve. She has become a daughter of Sarah. And as such, a woman steps into a new dimension of spiritual authority where she is able to destroy the inheritance of Eve inside of her, which is the inclination to rebellion. She is now able to please her husband, to please God, and to be His partner in church ministry. She has no limits to serve her Lord and Savior. She is heavenly dressed to minister. Glory to God for His wonderful and transforming grace!

## For Men Only

Marriage requires the death of both, man and woman, in order for the couple to experience the fullness of their relationship, as planned by God. This kind of death is required of man, following the example of Christ, who died for the church and gave Himself for her.

Peter concludes his instruction in the text we are studying with a direct commandment to husbands:

*Husbands, in the same way be considerate as you live with your wives, and treat them with respect as the weaker partner and as heirs with you of the gracious gift of life, so that nothing will hinder your prayers* (1 Pet. 3:7).

Husbands are supposed to live the daily life with spiritual discernment and respect for their wives. Discernment is a God-given gift for the family's government. Since husbands are watchers and leaders of their families, they should seek and discern Christ's direction for their decisions, for Christ is their Head. This is what their wives expect from them. When a woman trusts that Christ is the Head of her husband and she sees that he makes decisions in Christ, she has no problems in submitting to him. After all, they are both called to a common life and ministry under God's grace. Nothing should interfere or impede their marriage and mission in life from being fulfilled. Their prayers must not be interrupted because of the non-observance of these principles.

## Heirs of the Same Gracious Gift of Life

Peter says that man and woman are equals heirs of the same gracious gift of life. They should live their lives considering one another highly to keep their free access to God through prayer. He explains that an unstructured family life will affect the spiritual life of the couple. Their prayers and their intimacy with the Lord can be blocked. They are responsible to watch their relationship in order to keep their prayer access to God wide open and their spiritual authority for ministry flowing. Their prayers are intertwined. God will listen to the prayers of both or He will listen to none. At this point it is good to recall Paul's teaching: "*In the Lord, however, woman is not independent of man, nor is man independent of woman*" (1 Cor. 11:11). The most important lesson a couple has to learn, for the benefit of their family and of their ministerial life, is that submission precedes spiritual authority. So, if they want to reap the sheaves of spiritual authority in the lives of their children and their disciples, they first must sow the seeds of submission in the lives of their leaders — for "*a man reaps what he sows*" (Gal. 6: 7).

Women and men who understand and practice this principle will be able to freely obey this following commandment of the Lord: "All authority in heaven and on earth has been given to me. Therefore go and make disciples of all nations, baptizing them in the name of the Father and of the Son and of the Holy Spirit, and teaching them to obey everything I have commanded you. And surely I am with you always, to the very end of the age" (Mat. 28:18-20). May women and men give the honor, glory, and praise to Jesus Christ, the only Lord and Head of the church.

## Conclusion

# The Most Powerful Anointing Available

The spiritual key that releases and authorizes ministries for both men and women is submission. Jesus, the Son of God, and His submission to the Father is the supra example for all Christians. His submission was the foundation of the authority and power He received from God.

**Operation Submission for the Redemption of Humanity**

Jesus received the mission from God to save humanity from their sins. In order to do so, He became a man and a servant (Phil. 2:8). As a man, He needed to learn obedience to God to accomplish His mission.

*During the days of Jesus' life on earth, he offered up prayers and petitions with loud cries and tears to the one who could save him from death, and he was heard because of his reverent submission. Although he was a son, **he learned obedience** from what he suffered*

*and, once made perfect, he became the source of*
*eternal salvation for all who obey him* (Heb. 5: 7-9).

The Greek word *eulabeia*, translated as "reverent
submission" in verse 7, means "reverence" or "fear of God"
and refers to the perfect submission of the Son to the Father;
submission that guarantees that His prayers are heard by His
Father.[14] Jesus was completely submissive to the Father. In
His prayer at Gethsemane, the will of God prevailed (Lk. 22:
42). He learned obedience by submitting to the Father's will
and authority. He needed to learn obedience as the first-born
child of God as an example to His brothers and members of
the Body of Christ (Heb. 2: 9-12).

God's plan for the redemption of humanity has a strategic principle that first operated in Christ, who is the second
Adam. This principle is obedience to God. This principle is
central to all things in the Kingdom of God.

*For just as through the disobedience of the one man*
*the many were made sinners, so also* ***through the***
***obedience of the one man*** *the many will be made*
*righteous* (Rom. 5.19).

Sin entered the world through Adam; and death, the
result of sin, came to all men, for Adam is the father of
mankind (Rom. 5: 12). Jesus, the Head of a new kind of
people because of His obedience to God, extends His justice
to those who follow and obey Him.

## Operation Disobedience for the Rebellion of Humanity

It is clear since the beginning that Satan opposes God's
plan to redeem humanity from eternal death. His opposition originated in heaven when he rebelled against God and
took part of the angels with him. In the Garden of Eden,

he prepared a trap for Adam and Eve, and won a temporary victory when he witnessed their disobedience to God's commandment. God then announced His plan to restore humanity (Gen. 3:15).

Satan also tried to deceive Jesus by tempting Him in the desert with the intention to lead Him into rebellion against God (Mat. 4:8-10). As Satan's plan failed because Jesus was submissive to His Father, he instigated Judas to betray Jesus. That betrayal was not a surprise to Jesus, because the Scriptures foretold that the Son of God would be betrayed by someone called "the son of destruction" (Ps. 41:9; John 6:70, 71; 13:18; 17:12).

Again, Satan's plan failed because Christ's death was necessary for the redemption of humanity and He was obedient to God to the point of dying on the cross (Phil. 2:5-11; Heb. 2:9-10). In addition, Jesus was raised from the dead and was seated at the right hand of God in the heavenly places, "far above all rule and authority, power and dominion, and every title that can be given, not only in the present age but also in the one to come" (Eph. 1:21).

Satan's plan of opposition against the Church of Christ is denounced by the Apostle Paul in his second letter to the Thessalonians. Paul wanted to rectify the incorrect theology and in the life of the believers in Thessalonica. Many did not want to work anymore because they thought Jesus was about to return. Others affirmed that the Day of the Lord had already come and because of that, they were facing persecution and tribulations (2 Thess. 2:1- 2). Paul's exhortation is unequivocal:

*Don't let anyone deceive you in any way, for that day will not come until the rebellion occurs and the man of lawlessness is revealed the man doomed to destruction. He will oppose and will exalt himself over everything that is called God or is worshiped, so that he sets himself up in God's temple, proclaiming himself to be God* (2 Thess. 2:3-4).

Paul warns the Church that something serious and unprecedented will happen on earth as a sign to announce the second coming of Jesus. This sign is the Rebellion, with capital R, which will be headed by a rebellious man who will oppose the Church and the works of God. The plan of rebellion administered by Satan will have his culminating time with the uprising of a man he will equip. This man receives the same title Jesus' traitor had –the son of destruction (2 Thess. 2:3). This title is significant because it already establishes that he will not succeed, for he is doomed to destruction by our Lord Jesus Christ:

*And then the lawless one will be revealed whom the Lord Jesus will overthrow with the breath of his mouth and destroy by the splendor of his coming* (2 Thess. 2:8).

The purpose of this gigantic Rebellion will be to seat this lawless man in the Sanctuary of God. In order to accomplish it, Satan will empower his own man, trying to imitate God's plan.

*He will oppose and will exalt himself over everything that is called God or is worshiped, so that he sets himself up in God's temple, proclaiming himself to be God. ... The coming of the lawless one will be in accordance with the work of Satan displayed in all kinds of counterfeit miracles, signs and wonders, and in every sort of evil that deceives those who are perishing* (2 Thess. 2:4, 9-10).

This will be Satan's last attempt to deceive the peoples of the earth and take with him as many as he can to eternal destruction. The word that characterizes this man he will raise as his son is better rendered as the "lawless" or "out of law," meaning a man who does not submit to the Law of God. By his own nature he is rebellious to God and opposes everything that is God-related.

Satan will raise one as his own son (trying to imitate God the Father's strategy), who will operate counterfeit miracles, signs and wonders according to his own power. The purpose will be to deceive all humanity and have them follow him in his rebellion against God. Satan was not content in trying to raise the first Adam in disobedience to God; he tried to take Jesus, the second Adam into disobedience by tempting Him in the desert. He failed. Finally, he will raise his own man, the son of destruction, the son of rebellion.

This plan will seat this man in the sanctuary of God on earth. He will call himself "god" and will perform miracles to deceive many. The prophet Daniel and the Lord Jesus Christ announced the rising of this man (Dan. 11:36; Mat. 24:15). This plan of rebellion is identified by Paul as the "mystery of wickedness," which is already at work (2 Thess. 2:7). There is a dynamic in this mystery that Paul calls "powerful delusion." Those who are inclined towards injustice and disobedience against God will be susceptible to fall into this deception to follow this man and his rebellion. They will believe deception as truth. They will not be able to receive the love of God to be saved. They will be essentially rebellious people ... sons of rebellion.

This plan of rebellion is developing right now. It is possible to know some of its working, as we hear or read New Age preachers and writers. According to some of them, there are many children been born throughout the world with a supernatural level of understanding and intelligence, or a "higher self" as they explain it. According to their teaching, these children are expected to be the next level of human beings in the Evolutionist Process humanity has been undergoing for millenniums. They will be able to communicate with "superior beings" that now can only be seen in "shadow" and by one's peripheral vision. They are referred to as "shadow figures" or "shadow beings". These children's mothers have either been visited by extraterrestrials beings or felt anything unusual during their pregnancy. Books, courses, and seminars are being offered to help the parents of such children to know how to raise them and develop their "higher self". According to this teaching, these children will be capable of operating in a supernatural level that they call "magic" and perform many miraculous and extraordinary signs. This is the spirit of the antichrist preparing the scenario for the temporary government of the Antichrist, who may very well be already born. Isn't this what the apostle Paul warned us about?

*Don't you remember that when I was with you I used to tell you these things? And now you know what is holding him back, so that he may be revealed at the proper time. For the secret power of lawlessness is already at work; but the one who now holds it back will continue to do so till he is taken out of the way. And then the lawless one will be revealed whom the Lord Jesus will overthrow with the breath of his mouth and destroy by the splendor of his coming. The coming of the lawless one will be in accordance with the work of Satan displayed in all kinds of counterfeit miracles, signs and wonders, and in every sort of evil that deceives those who are perishing. They perish because they refused to love the truth and so be saved. For this reason God sends them a powerful delusion so that they will believe the lie and so that all will be condemned who have not believed the truth but have delighted in wickedness* (2 Thess. 2: 7-12).

## Disobedience: the Nature of the Sons of Rebellion

What is the importance of the apostle Paul's warning for the purpose of this book? As we mentioned, the plan for the great rebellion is already at work in the world. Each day we see its progress in all humanity. All the systems of the world, under the leadership of the "prince of this world" are being strategically organized in order to be ready for the final phase when the lawless man will be manifested and believed by those who are inclined to deception.

Satan's plan is for humanity to intensify its level of rebellion against God to the point that their hearts become vulnerable and they will be attracted and seduced by the lawless and rebellious man. He will be the hero for rebels and the sons of disobedience, those who believe the deception.

We are living in exciting and crucial prophetic times. This generation may just witness the revelation of the man of iniquity and the Rapture of the Church.

## Submission: the Nature of the Sons of Redemption

Thank God, the plan of redemption is also at work in the world and opposes and prevents the advancement of the plan of rebellion by making disciples and sons of obedience for Jesus Christ. The plan of redemption, carried out by Jesus through His submission to the Father, continues to work in the world through the Church, formed by the redeemed who obey His Word and are submissive to His voice.

The greatest distinction between the participants of the plan of redemption and the plan of rebellion is the *submissive* inclination of their hearts.

We want to present this eschatological picture at the conclusion of this book to make it clear that submission is a characteristic outflow of the people of God redeemed by the Blood of Jesus and transformed by the Holy Spirit to live as sons of God in the midst of a rebellious generation. This kind of submission is reflected in all the relationships of the redeemed: with God, with Christ, with the Holy Spirit, with spiritual leaders, with authorities, with parents, with husbands, and with all the members of the Body of Christ.

Submission is not a manipulative or controlling action, although many people want to use it this way. It is a word that expresses the very nature of a people redeemed by Christ to live as sons of obedience towards God and each other, in love. This makes a remarkable contrast to the sons of disobedience, who walk under the dominion of the prince of this world, the father of rebellion.

## The Most Powerful Weapon against the Plan of Rebellion

There is a spiritual weapon given to the Church of Christ that powerfully thwarts with the plan of rebellion at work in the world. The apostle Paul reveals this secret and lethal weapon in the following text:

*The weapons we fight with are not the weapons of the world. On the contrary, they have divine power to demolish strongholds. We demolish arguments and every pretension that sets itself up against the knowledge of God, and we take captive every thought to make it obedient to Christ. And we will be ready to punish every act of disobedience, once your obedience is complete* (2 Cor. 10:4-6).

When the Church learns how to live according to the law of submission in Christ, it will also be able to destroy the power of rebellion and to punish disobedience in the hearts of people who are rebellious against God. Every thought will be taken captive to the obedience of Christ. This means that the more we are submissive in our lives, the more spiritual authority we will have to defeat Satan's schemes and to demolish his strongholds that work against the redemptive plan of God. The more submissive we are the more spiritual authority we will have to win the peoples of the earth for Christ. Submission is a spiritual weapon of unequalled power for the Church of Christ in the spiritual warfare.

All men and women, of every age, civil status, color, race or culture, are enrolled in the school of life learning the important lesson of submission to Christ. In their diverse situations of life they are given opportunities to learn this lesson. Children learn submission in their parent's school; wives in their husband's; citizens in their government authorities'; servants and employees in their bosses', and sheep in their pastor's school. We all should be aware that it is imperative to be approved and to learn submission in order to be prepared to exert the spiritual authority needed to minister in God's House and in the world.

Submission releases the authority, the power and the anointing of God for both, men and women, to serve as ministers in the Body of Christ. This is the most powerful anointing available on earth. The Church must learn submission as soon as possible. At any cost!

*I pray that Jesus will reveal this deep truth to His whole Church in the face of the earth. And that a submissive generation of people will arise to serve Him with all their hearts, their determination and willingness, and so unconditionally to the point they will obstruct the progress of Satan's plans in the world.*

*I pray that God's people will have a lifestyle of obedience that will be so attractive to others billions of the peoples of the earth in such a way, that when this lawless man, the son of rebellion, appears, he will be disappointed to find only a few rebels to follow him and worship him and believe in his lies.*

*I pray that the Church throughout the earth will understand the importance of the time we live in, and the significance of this anointing that will come only through real submission to Christ. This will be an unprecedented anointing that the Church and the earth has not yet seen. It will be the anointing of the Bride of Christ being prepared to see her Bridegroom. The Church will experience a power that will bring about a great harvest for Christ.*

*For the Word of God says: This is good, and pleases God our Savior, who wants all men to be saved and to come to the knowledge of the truth (1 Tim.2:4).*

*Respectfully and prayerfully submitted to the Body of Christ.*

*Izes Calheiros*

# END NOTES AND REFERENCES

1 Estevan Voth, *Comentario Bíblico Hispano- Americano*, Miami, Editorial Caribe, 1992, p. 80 (Génesis, primera parte). Translation by the author.

2 To better understand these interpretations, see the analysis by Ruth A. Tucker in her book *Women in the maze: questions and answers on biblical equality*, Illinois Inter Varsity, 1992, p. 35.

3This verse presents the first occurrence of poetry in the Old Testament, according to the NIV Study Bible, Zondervan Publishing House, Grand Rapids, MI, 1973. Comments on Genesis 1. 27.

4 Synonymic parallelism is the repetition of a phrase or a stanza with the same meaning, even if with different words, of the previous phrase or a stanza. The Book of Job contains many examples of this type of parallelism.

5 Jerome Smith, *The new Treasure of Scriptural Knowledge*, Nashville, Thomas Nelson, 1992, p. 4. Comments on Genesis 1. 27.

6 Caio Fabio D'Araujo Filho, *A mulher no projeto do reino de Deus*, Rio de Janeiro, Vinde, 1997, p. 21.

7 David Prior, *Mensagem de 1 Coríntios (The Message of 1 Corinthians)*, São Paulo, ABU, 1985, p. 194.

8 David Prior, 1985, p. 11.

9 *Bíblia Sagrada*, 2. Edição Revista e Atualizada no Brasil, São Paulo, Sociedade Bíblica do Brasil, 1993, p. 205.

10 These are the biblical references: Acts 8:1; 11: 27-30; 13:1-3; 14:23; 15:2, 4, 6, 22-23; 16:4; 20:17, 28; 21:17-18; 1 Tim. 5:17; Tit.1:5; Jas. 5:14; 1 Pet. 5:1, among other texts.

11 Footnote: For this discussion we are using the term sexist to refer to any decisions or assignment of rules in the church based upon gender alone.

12 John Kohlenberger III, org., *The Greek New Testament*. Grand Rapids, Zondervan, 1993, p. 384.

13 For a biblical understanding of *submission* refer to pg. 11 on this book.

14 Russell P. Shedd, editor, *Bíblia Shedd*, São Paulo, Editora Vida Nova, 1998, p. 1711, s. v. Commentary on Hebrews 5.7.

CPSIA information can be obtained at www.ICGtesting.com
Printed in the USA
LVOW06s0850230714

395639LV00001B/1/P